TALKING *with* GOD

J. Ben Pickering

ZENAN
Media & Publishing

Published in Melbourne, Australia
By Zenan Media and Publishing. 2014

Zenan Media & Publishing
P.O. Box 3143
Ivanhoe North
Victoria. 3079

© J. Ben Pickering 2013

By This Author:
- From Hate To Hope – The Vision of Obadiah
- Twelve Stones – The Breastplate
- The Shekhinah Glory
- I Think I've Burnt My Bushel!
- The Little Book of Talking With God
- Talking With God
- 52 Memorial Moments
- Jesus among the Gentiles

ISBN
978-0-9578006-7-0

This book is dedicated to:

A faithful and tenacious team of proofreaders who wrestle my turn of phrase into something resembling language. Their patience, wisdom, guidance and general grasp of grammar (it's something to do with writing apparently, they insist on it anyway), eventually make these thoughts and words comprehendible.

A lot of editing goes into writing, far more than I think is necessary – this and other books would never see the light of day if it wasn't for the great kindness shown by:

Bev, Carol, Jean, Lainy, Robin and Sue.

A big **'Thank you'** to each of you. Your love and inspiration means a lot to so many people. We all owe you much recognition for what you do so well with such good grace.

TALKING
with
GOD

Hallowed Ground

Step light on hallowed ground
Feel its eyes on you, hear its sound
Listen to earth, know that soil
Reared in blood, grown in toil.

Summers, winters, past and long gone
Tell in it what was there done
In the name of hope it died, it rose
And lives forever, in all it grows.

Touched by hands that fed its yearning
Taught those few that cared for learning
Sprig sprung in dusty ground of note
Reap and sow and reap again – with hope.

~ Cheltenham
October 2001

Contents...

Foreword...	...8
Introduction...	...10
Talking with God...	...13
Praise with God ...	...39
Reflection with God...	...79
Petition with God...	...116
Answers with God...	...146

Foreword

By Robert J Lloyd

Effectual & fervent Prayer

I recall the story about the man who explained that he prayed while driving his car - and his wife sitting at his side remarked, 'So do I!'

God knows where we are at all times and it is impossible to be somewhere that God is not. Even down in the belly of the fish Jonah knew that God was there too. Since God is everywhere by his Spirit so we can be everywhere by our prayers.

Paul tells us *to 'Pray without ceasing.'* Some versions say *'constantly'* or *'continually'*. We never really appreciated how this was possible until we read JB's book, "Talking with God."

It really opens our eyes to understanding this as he explains to us how to live in a circle of prayer, so that in a sense we are surrounded by God's love at all times and we are actually living *in* prayer all the time.

Jesus often spent the entire night in prayer to his Heavenly Father and we should go to bed with a prayer in our mind and wake up praying.

We like to drift off into sleep using the words of Isaiah *'Thou dost keep him in perfect peace, whose mind is stayed on thee, because he trusts in thee. Trust in the LORD for ever, for the LORD GOD is an everlasting rock.'*

And we like to wake up reciting to our Heavenly Father the words of David, *'This is the day which the LORD hath made; we will rejoice and be glad in it.'*

JB recommends that each of us should make our own written prayer list and use it daily to be sure that we pray for all those people we know who are in need of our prayers.

When Jesus knew that Peter was going to deny him three times he prayed to his Heavenly Father for Peter; and told Peter he had been praying for him. Peter thought that he would never deny Jesus but he did. Perhaps if while he was spending those few hours in the Garden with Jesus he had been praying instead of sleeping, might he then been able to resist this? Later he was very bold and took out his sword to defend his Lord from a mob of armed soldiers when he was hopelessly outnumbered. Jesus stepped forward and healed the victim to prevent Peter himself from being slain right at that moment and it was a lesson for Peter.

We highly recommend this book to everyone. Prayer is such a wonderful gift from God to each of us and this book will help us appreciate it more - and make *personal prayer* the very focus of our lives.

Reading this book will inspire you to make your prayers enthusiastic and meaningful in your everyday workaday lives. The Apostle James tells us that our prayers should be fervent as well as effective. *'The effectual fervent prayer of a righteous man availeth much.'*

May this book help each of us to be more fervent in our own prayer lives.

Robert J Lloyd

Introduction

Some years ago we published a cute little book entitled, 'The Little Book of Talking with God'. This began life as a list of quotes from the Bible and from other people throughout history who had something brief and profound to say about prayer. The idea of making these notes into a little book soon came along.

Initially the little book was meant to be a pocket reminder on aspects of prayer. We accidentally printed what we thought would be far too many copies than we would need – after all, how many people would actually carry this book around in their pocket? I mean these pockets were already full of wallets, purses, mobile phones and the odd handkerchief or two.

With the kind assistance of an able illustrator and animator in Lucy Dangerfield we added a couple of small illustrations. At Lucy's suggestion we added an animation that worked as one 'flicked' though the pages of the book. This proved to be a stroke of genius on her part – people would show others the quirky little animation – and they wanted a little book too!

What surprised us most about 'The Little Book of Talking with God' was how often people bought multiple copies. One day a lady bought twelve at once, and when asked how many pockets she had she replied, "Oh no, I use them instead of gift cards. There's more great quotes in here that I want to share than I'll ever get in a gift card!"

This together with other feedback made it apparent that the little book had found a new and more important role – it had become an effective preaching tool. The little book was just a bit of fun to begin with but it seemed to decide for itself what it would be and where it would go – and even at times how it would get there.

'The Little Book of Talking with God' started turning up all over the world, and people sent photos of themselves and the little book in different places. Someone actually sent a photo of their cat, fast asleep and clutching a copy of the Little Book - we certainly didn't see that one coming.

However, the majority of the feedback was that people wanted more information on this approach to understanding prayer. The original quotes were only meant to be thought starters and prompts for discussion. So the more these requests for more information arrived the more seriously it was being taken that there was a genuine need for 'The Little BIGGER Book of Talking with God'. So after some gentle arm-twisting, some hours in study, prayer and meditation we finally introduce for you here – 'Talking with God'.

My personal prayer is that you will enjoy the thoughts and ideas in here. The format has deliberately been designed to make prayer easy to understand – but also to make it evident that there is a wealth of spiritual thought that you can add for yourself.

May God bless you and help you in your life, especially your *prayer life* as you grow in peace, grace, understanding and the hope of the promise of eternity.

Your friend in this journey,

JBP

~ 1 ~
TALKING *with* GOD

A gift, the beginning of a journey

There are several objectives that we want to achieve in this book; the dominant one on our agenda is to develop not just a simple understanding of prayer but how to *live* a Prayer Life.

That may sound like a big challenge – and to some degree it is. But it is not beyond any of us to achieve this; it just depends on how we approach it. The basis for our approach to this subject is because we want to learn more than just what someone else said about prayer. We don't want to look at every specific example of prayer, even though we have an abundance of these in Scripture.

At the outset of this journey, it's important to remember that prayer is not a talisman, it is not a good-luck charm. It's not something we only use when we find ourselves in trouble or don't know what to do next. Instead we want turn the tables on this perception. We don't want to just say, 'we can pray' or that 'we can *use* prayer' - instead we actually want to appreciate that we can '*live* prayer'.

And so, to do this we are broadly going step by step through five sections of what it takes to live a life of prayer, and for prayer to be a greater part of our existence. We'll use these sections:
- Talking with God
- Praise with God
- Reflection with God
- Petition with God
- Answers with God

And so as we take this journey together we ask that you to put your mind in the direction which this subject takes us and embrace the desire to talk with God - to practise and pray with a confidence that prayer was *prepared* especially for us.

You see, prayer is a gift - every time we pray we should remember this. It is a gift to the young, to the old, it is a gift to the free, it is a gift to those not so. Prayer has no national boundaries, it respects no borders, it has only the limitations we put upon it – particularly when we don't understand the reason why God really designed it.

It really is something absolutely phenomenal – it is a gift beyond anything you have ever received in your life. Granted, you and I both have our special moments, moments that we remember in our lives that were simply grand – yet I challenge you at this time to reflect, indeed to remember that you have received no gift more interesting than prayer.

Prayer is the ability to speak with the Almighty, to converse with the Eternal - because prayer *is* talking with God.

Prayer positions us within God's will

Prayer positions us in our relationship with our Heavenly Father and it gives us confidence and knowledge that He is not so far removed. When used often and with knowledge, prayer is a reset switch which works on a divine logic and always achieves a divine equilibrium – which means it doesn't work at extremes that make no sense. By its very nature prayer has to make sense of everything; God who is everywhere and knows everything made it so.

We know of the omnipresence of God. Recently I was discussing this with my brother and we were talking about how God can seem so close to us at times. And that He really fills this great void constantly as we go about our daily lives. This is what we want to bring out as we discuss talking with God and living a life of prayer. In fact, we can contribute to the consistency of filling that void by becoming people who live not just average lives – but lives of prayer.

You know as well as I do that there are times when we pray to God for praise, for reflection or petition and we may feel that sometimes petitions go unanswered but we will address this issue a little later. Remember that when we pray to our Heavenly Father we *are* talking with God, not metaphorically or figuratively or symbolically – but literally and in reality.

When we talk with God we need to bear in mind that He hears everything we say. Not just some of what we say just when it suits Him – He hears everything we say. As we grow to understand that God always hears prayers, we'll realise how these times of talking with God also need to relate to His will.

I remember the story of a little assembly that every year had a Sunday School picnic and every year the Sunday School superintendant would announce that the picnic could occur on such and such a date. A dear old sister who was a member of the assembly would every year faithfully pray for good weather for the picnic. As far as everybody else in the assembly was concerned this was quite a worry, because almost every year it rained!

So, one year the superintendant, well aware of this probably happening, decided to get smart and went to the sister a couple of weeks before announcing the date of the picnic and said, 'Dear sister, I suppose you are going to pray that we have good weather for the Sunday School picnic this year?' The old sister with a twinkle in her eye replied, 'No brother. I've decided that this year I'm going to pray for *you* and that you may have the good sense to pick the right day for the Sunday School picnic!'

You see, prayer positions us in God's will. The sister, realising from observation that it wasn't good weather that was needed; changed her prayer to what she knew was more likely to be within the will of God. One may wonder why she didn't take this approach earlier. However, I dare say she taught the brother an important lesson.

Praise-Reflection-Petition

Prayer is for praise. Prayer is for reflection. Prayer is for petition. Praise-Reflection-Petition. Whenever we speak to God in prayer, that is whenever we talk with God; anything we say to Him in prayer will fall into one of these three categories.

Some people may like to look at this differently or perhaps add categories. One may declare, 'Well there's petition but there's also intercession.' And yes, we can have intercession in prayer. But frankly, when we make an addition such as intercession it is really just another form of petition.

Also, quite rightly, we may say that prayer should always include a request for the forgiveness of our sins. We should always reflect on our nature and what we've done and if you are like me, quite often what we should not have done. But again, this is still reflection. And if we seek forgiveness – isn't the act of *requesting it* an obvious form of petition?

So basically, in talking with God we have these three elements that form the structure of prayer. You will find them in many prayers in Scripture, particularly Christ's prayers. All the phrases we can imagine to use in prayer will fall into the category of either praise, reflection or petition.

As an exercise; think about the last prayer you prayed. If you can't remember that too well, then close your eyes for a few moments and say a prayer right now.

Now you've done that, think back – can you see the expressions of praise, which thoughts were reflection, which requests were of petition?

Maybe you realised that your brief prayer contained phrases you often use in prayer – sometimes this is good. But maybe, like me, you realised that you use some phrases more often than you actually think about them. They can roll off the tongue because they are familiar instead of heart-felt.

What was the balance of your prayer? Was there more of one category than another? Don't worry if there was, although balance may lead to a healthy prayer life on the whole; the fact is that there are times when one category is more important than another. Overall it should balance out, especially when you can distinguish the differences between praise, reflection and petition.

This little exercise, combined with the simple knowledge of the types of expression in talking with God is a good way to see how prayer works, how we can improve these different components of our communication – and therefore understand and respect our time talking with God.

Let's take a moment to think about another prayer. Take an example from daily life – for instance the prayer before a meal. Can you see the elements of praise, reflection and petition? Perhaps it goes something like this;

- Thanking God for the blessing of food – that's praise.
- Remembering how He has blessed the earth with food – that's reflection.
- Asking that the strength you receive from the blessing of food will be used wisely in His service – that's petition because you are asking for something according to His will.

Try another prayer you remember, perhaps one that is required during a Sunday service, at a wedding, at a funeral, at a child's bedtime.

Another thing you will want to try soon is if you can make a whole prayer with just *one* category! This is very interesting and leads to an effective understanding – it's a very powerful exercise when it comes to including and appreciating all three categories in a longer prayer.

The act of articulating stimulates our mind

Praying, particularly out loud, even if only with a soft voice, helps us to think about praise; to reflect on those things that our Father has done for us. It also focuses our thoughts as to what we should be doing for Him as His sons and daughters. Such thinking gets our minds *working out* what we really want and what we see that we need – and expressing those things.

A friend and avid Bible scholar wrote this to me recently and I think she is absolutely right, "Praying aloud is powerful indeed. I think when we hear the words we are praying it's an affirmation of our intent, kind of like typing something in capital letters. It doesn't matter that no one hears except you than God - who else needs to hear anyway?!"

Praying aloud (or under our breath if necessary) is *a lot* different from talking to God in our head. The reason is that there is, despite what anyone jokingly asserts, much going on in our heads. There are happy things, sad things, things we are excited about, worried about, fears, concerns and memories both good and bad. Our minds are never still; our nature allows no vacuum.

Talking separates the layers and frees what we want to speak about with God. If we pray just in our head for something, it is extremely easy for the pathways of the mind, our thought patterns to link-up and run to thoughts that are not relevant at the time. This takes us away from our purpose.

Often we can just trundle through life feeling that we want this or need that but when we go to God in prayer, we have an opportunity to refine and discern what is really important. We get to ask God, 'Do you want this for me?' We don't do that if we don't pray. We just feel hungry so we eat, we just feel tired so we sleep. But when we are praying, when we live a prayer life, we articulate sentiment beyond the powerlessness of feelings themselves.

Even writing this is an exercise in articulation. I haven't got a note down about every sentence I intended to write for you before I started; if I did then this would pretty much be written before it was written! Instead, having familiarised myself with the subject over some time and having reflected on it in a number of ways – I can go ahead and tell you what I think is important about this subject without any special limits and without having to think of something remarkably new.

You know what it is like when you are discussing something with friends around the dinner table. You range across whatever topics are relevant at the time and while explaining a subject to your friends it suddenly dawns on you that there is something so big, so important, such an interesting point that you wonder why you haven't thought of it before - despite the fact that you have reflected on it many times before. We say it just 'pops into our head.' Why does this happen? Because *articulating* makes it happen!

When we open our mouths and start to talk about what we really want to say we have to think about it that little bit more than if we simply turn it over in our minds. Why? Because our minds desire to be stimulated by *action* – and talking *is* an action. It's not just a method for focusing our communication. It's more than that and the most important thing that articulation does is fulfil an absolute requirement for prayer because...

Prayer is an act

Prayer is not a thought or a fuzzy feeling or a comfortable warm glow. Prayer is an act. So opening our mouths and speaking with God brings our minds into play. Imagine for a moment what it would be like to live your whole life 'in play'. Not on the periphery of divine consciousness but actually *participating in* prayer.

Imagine living your whole life as a son or daughter, a friend of the Living God – who doesn't just think or feel but who speaks and acts. Now we see that the more we pray, the more we act, and the closer we *are* in our relationship with God. Would you like to live like that all day, every day? What is stopping you?

The answer is actually, 'nothing'. Of course, God doesn't need rambling, meaningless nonsense – to be honest He's been hearing that from 'professors' of faith for thousands of years.

So, we can be fairly confident He won't mind hearing a more sincere attempt from you or me! If someone is honestly approaching Him to learn more and communicate more there are hundreds of examples of His willingness to hear and to help us become better communicators near His level.

As we develop in confidence and our understanding of prayer, there will come a time when we will actually find ourselves talking with God over some of the smallest things at the strangest moments. When this happens, don't worry, you're not going mad – you are just arriving in a space that means things are coming together for you in communicating with God. That's what He made prayer for.

Prayer and God's will

Prayer directly corresponds to your relationship with God. This is where it comes back to praying, communicating and *articulating* to God things that concern His will and that concern our relationship with Him. God's will is important when we consider prayer.

Do you know God's will? Open your Bible to 1 John 5:

> "I write these things to you who believe in the name of the Son of God that you may ***know*** that you have eternal life. And this is the confidence that we have toward him, that if we ask ***anything*** according to his will he hears us. And if we know that he hears us in ***whatever we ask***, we ***know*** that we ***have*** the requests that we have asked of him."

In considering this quote doesn't that make our grip on talking to God more powerful? We understand talking with God a little more.

God is a lot of things; a God of love, jealousy and many, many more attributes – importantly one of these is that He very willing. Bear this in mind when you talk with God.

Prayer is not about overriding God's reluctance – prayer is rather taking hold of God's willingness and understanding His will. Of course, to this end, the Bible is His ultimate guide for us. Consider these words from Psalm 119:

> "Oh how I love your law! It is my meditation all the day. Your commandment makes me wiser than my enemies, for it is ever with me. I have more understanding than all my teachers, for your testimonies are my meditation. I understand more than the aged, for I keep your precepts. I hold back my feet from every evil way, in order to keep your word. I do not turn aside from your rules, for you have taught me. How sweet are your words to my taste, sweeter than honey to my mouth! Through your precepts I get understanding; therefore I hate every false way. Your word is a lamp to my feet and a light to my path."

So guidance such as this is what we receive when we call in the will of God. There is so much in the Scriptures. I know for myself every time I open the Word of God I find something new and am continually surprised at the depths one can go to. It's simply inexhaustible - and in it is God's will.

Talk with God all day

Going back to the point we made before in Psalm 119 – talk with God all day - I don't know if we can over-emphasise this. Is there anything in your day you don't want to share with God? If not, share it with God and talk with Him all day. Say 'thank you' for the small things. Ask for guidance in small things.

There's nothing wrong with saying, 'God, I'm absolutely sure I'm going to have a tough day at work today, please be with me.' Then halfway to work, whether you drive or catch a bus, pray again, 'Thank you God, I'm feeling more confident about the tough day I have ahead of me, but please be with me.'

God *never* tires of hearing from you. Just like a parent never grows weary of the sound of their child's voice. Well, perhaps that's not entirely true but when all goes quiet and you can't hear the kids - you do start wondering what is going on! When you can hear the child you know where the child is, what the child is doing and/or feeling, you relax because you expect that all is well. And just as importantly the child knows that the parent knows.

Our Heavenly Father is different from parents as we know them but He does know our thoughts, He knows how we feel and He does know our worries and our cares. And just like the child knows that the parent knows where he or she is at – so God wishes us also to be comfortable in the knowledge that He knows where we are.

He wants to hear us so that we also know that He can hear us – and then become comfortable in the relationship as He always is. He doesn't want us complacent in the relationship – but He does want us content and He does want us to trust Him. We have nothing to hide; there is nothing we can hide even if we want to, so talk a little more with God – and often.

Don't for one moment think I'm good at this; I have my good days and bad ones. I have moments, sometimes very long ones in between talking with God. But at the end of a day I can always tell when I think I've shared enough of it with God in prayer. It's a matter of forming a healthy habit which stays with you for your whole life.

In Psalm 119, a little further on from where we read earlier we notice this phrase:

> "Seven times a day I praise you for your righteous rules."

Seven times a day! How many times have we perhaps prayed today? Well, let's add them up... once for breakfast, once for lunch, once for dinner and probably pray once more before we go to sleep. OK, that's four times. Is that standard? Or perhaps we should ask a harder question – are we happy with that?

'Seven times a day I praise you for your righteous rules,' the Psalmist wrote. He doesn't say once a day I praise you, once for breakky, once for tiffin, once for tucker and once for whatever else I forgot to praise you for today. He says seven times a day I praise you *just* for your righteous rules - *just* for God's laws. He doesn't say, 'I praise you once for A, B, C, D, E, F, and G.' He says seven times a day he *just* prays for 'A'.

And notice what his prayer is – it's *just for praise*. He hasn't even told us yet how many times a day he prays with reflection or petition. It's not that David has set an impossible standard we can never achieve – instead he's given us the inspiration to make the opportunity to do the same and more! So, what are we doing in our prayer life?

To have a prayer life doesn't mean prayers have to be long. We can't all be prayer warriors on the same level as David (and don't look at me - I know I'm not!). And likewise we're not saying we have to pray seven times a day for one thing, but if that's what it takes for us to properly articulate our praise, our reflection or our petition to God then sure, do it seven times or more if you like.

In fact, I dare say that the Lord Jesus wouldn't mind mediating something we ask in his name *seventy times seven* if that's what we feel it takes to express ourselves to God. Seven in this verse is more than a number, it suggests completeness. It's an expression of completely praying something out.

Make a prayer list

Today we may have prayed for things that we have been mindful of, things we have heard about or affect us. We may have prayed for brother So and so, sister Such and such, for the peace of Jerusalem and for the Master to return soon, for forgiveness of our sins, for those nearby and those afar. We also pray for our families, friends and loved ones. That's quite a growing prayer list already. Do you have a prayer list?

Start a prayer list today if you haven't already! It's yours and you can do whatever you like with it - but use it to pray. Keep it on a little slip of paper in your purse or your wallet and carry it with you. You can add to it anytime you like. And you can tick off the things that no longer need prayer. It's yours so you can use it and manage it however you want.

A practical way of managing a prayer list is to have a *masterlist* in a convenient place where you have time to concentrate on items to go on your list. From that make a list you can carry with you wherever you go. Is it going to be hard to remember to take it with you? Well, when's the last time you left home without your wallet/purse or mobile phone? You won't forget them so keep a list in your wallet or purse, or even on your phone so you can take it out wherever you go.

A simple way to do this is with a piece of paper you can fold in three. If you need specific directions: Take a DL slip of paper (that's one third of an A4 sheet) and fold it into three sections – now you've made a little booklet 7cm by 10cm (3" by 4"). It's easy to fit this in any wallet, purse or pocket – and there's plenty of room to make your list and it's always with you. And don't forget you'll also need a small pencil too!

These days people increasingly keep notes on their mobile devices. It's easy to use these as places to keep your prayer list. God doesn't mind where you list what you pray for, it's *your* reminder – He doesn't need reminding.

It's important to do this if you have a memory like mine. I'll talk to someone, discover a certain need and at the late hour when I am getting into bed, I forget about the need. Sometimes I'm too tired to even think about my own. But that doesn't happen if I have a prayer list.

Try keeping a big prayer list in your home. My mother keeps a big one on a white-board on her refrigerator. She lives a long way away from me so I don't see how often she updates it. But when I visit it's strange, in a nice sort of way, to see my name on the fridge - and it being there doesn't even have anything to do with food.

Perhaps keep a big prayer list on your desk at work – there's a lot of people out there, believe me, who want to understand prayer. When people at work know you keep a regular prayer list you sure get a lot of visitors!

Many people don't understand this gift of prayer, and you know what? They need *you* to pray for them. They *want* you to pray for them. They feel blessed and special that you can do something for them that they feel inadequate doing themselves.

This may sound like something that's a bit too far out there for you. Some people just don't want to or don't feel comfortable demonstrating their faith openly. I really understand this as I have been there too. But prayer is powerful, really powerful and in so many ways.

It is standard practice when out to lunch with people I work with, no one touches their plate until I've said a prayer – they really love this. It makes them feel special in a novel way. And of course it's always fun to pretend I have an important distraction like a message on my phone or something just as the plates hit the table! Well, sometimes I have to make my own fun.

People who know and trust you generally respect you too. I can tell you from experience that People I work with genuinely love to have a prayer said for them. Even if they're not 'religious' they still appreciate it when they know they are included in your prayers.

Another situation that arises from a prayer list at work is that I sometimes get asked to pray for people I don't even know! "Hi JB, can you pray for my Mum, she's going in for an operation tomorrow." And does this change my prayer practise? You bet it does!

Another modern take on the prayer list is email. Try this idea too. Use a webmail provider and create a prayer list *folder*. The grapevine is already well established with this medium so it takes no effort at all to add to the list – you just save the emails everyone sends you in your prayer folder. If you don't receive an email about things you want to pray for you just send yourself an email and add it to the list. From then on you can just add or delete as you need to. And, even better, you can print the screen and then put it in your pocket.

As you can see, there are many ideas we can use!

What about those who do share your interest and understanding of prayer, or those who you don't know whether they do or not? Take Sister Anne for example - she needs a prayer for… I don't know what she needs a prayer for but I'm sure it's something. Brother Bill, he needs a prayer for something too – what does Brother Bill need a prayer for? You see, with a prayer list we also get to see who is not on the list and then we can find some reason to add them.

Finding problems or needs that require prayer is quite an adventure in itself. Brother Jim has a problem – but I don't know what his problem is, but I can still pray for help with his problem. I don't have to know all the details; God does. And I can also just thank God for Brother Jim. Maybe I'll just thank God that Jim is a part of my life in Christ. I may not have much to do with Jim but now I am glad that he made it onto my prayer list. It changes *me* as much as my prayers can change things for him.

Are you getting the idea? Right; a prayer list has become more powerful than just a plain list of things – it's a tool to effectively live a great prayer life and to grow our understanding. This is how prayer *changes* our mind and really transforms our life!

If we don't use a prayer list we are doing one of two things: either we're forgetting a lot of people (including ourselves!) or we are relying on an unbelievable memory. We are either able to think about a lot of things that God has given us and that we receive or we are forgetting to ask or thank God for a lot of things that we haven't thought through properly yet – and of course, not yet articulated in praise, reflection or petition - all because they were not on the list!

This is called the 'Prayer of the Special Common.' I repeat it here because it brings out a couple of things that you might want to put on your prayer list to start with. And notice that the items on this list may not seem super-important – but imagine being without them! It goes like this:

> LORD, thank you for this sink full of dirty dishes – we had food to eat.
> Thank you for an unmade bed – it was very comfortable last night.
> Thank you for this heap of soiled laundry – we have good, warm clothes.
> Thank you for the bathroom, complete with spattered mirror, soggy towels, grimy sink and an assortment of clothes thrown at (not in) the clothes hamper – it's still very convenient.
> Thank you for the finger-smudged refrigerator – it has served us faithfully for years. Inside are cool drinks and enough leftovers for another meal.
> Thank you for this oven that must be cleaned today - it has baked many goodies to perfection or close to it.
> Thank you for the leaves out there in the yard that need raking – we enjoy the private yard.

Thank you for that slamming screen-door – the children are healthy and able to run and play.
LORD the presence of all these chores awaiting me today says that you have richly blessed this family.
I shall do them gratefully and cheerfully.
I thank you through the example of your Son, Amen.

Along with a prayer list the more creative of you may like to start a prayer journal. Or perhaps even a prayer scrapbook, pick up pieces of anything that you hear or see about prayer and include them. Illustrate them – make them yours, you can write your own book about prayer!

Pray wherever you are

Pray when travelling. It's prime prayer time – we've got nothing else to do. Sure, we can take along a book or a newspaper but we can also use the *spare* time in prayer. If you are standing in the queue at the bank for instance, use that time for prayer. A queue moves so much faster when we use the time to pray. We have so many examples of these snippets of time in our lives. Pray wherever and whenever you can.

Martin Luther is credited with having once said,

> "I have so much to do that I must spend the first three hours of each day in prayer."

I don't get up that early! But if I did, could I spend three hours in prayer? I don't know if Martin Luther really did either. I don't know if I could keep that kind of regime up very long. But I know I've got a lot to do today, a lot more to do before I go to bed. It's important to *make* time in our day to pray.

When you can, find a comfortable place to pray. Shut out those things that you don't need. These times are very precious. I once knew a sister who had such a place which she called her 'prayer corner' – I never saw her use it but I can imagine it was the perfect place to stop and talk with God. It was simply a comfortable chair situated near the window overlooking her garden. Next to the chair was a little table which I could imagine supporting a hot cup of tea or coffee, and probably her prayer list. It seemed an ideal place to me.

Her habit was that her husband having left for work and she having dropped their children at school, she would take time in her 'prayer corner' before tackling the weightier work of the day. Sound good? Try it.

Why not spend time with someone who cares as much about prayer as you do? Ask them to pray with you.

Pray on a mountain top; we know Jesus did that often. You can find him up there in Luke chapter 6 and again in chapter 9 for instance. In his day they were places of quiet because people didn't usually live on top of mountains – it was too much effort to carry everything up and down. We drive up mountains now, but back then there were less crowds in the clouds, so to speak. One thing that hasn't changed however is that mountains still offer inspiring views, where we can take in the grandeur of creation and reflect on the hand of God.

Pray by candlelight as David did. In Psalm 42 he wrote;

> "By day the LORD commands his steadfast love, and at night his song is with me, a prayer to the God of my life."

If we have a prayer life – we have a God of our life too. And that's how it affects us, just as it affected David.

Pray in a loud place. We can do that – it opens up so many more opportunities for prayer when we can pray in a loud place. Have a look at 1 Chronicles 5, which is a time early in the establishment of God's people in the Promised Land;

> "They waged war against the Hagrites, Jetur, Naphish, and Nodab. And when they prevailed over them, the Hagrites and all who were with them were given into their hands, for they cried out to God in the battle, and he granted their urgent plea because they trusted in him."

Notice that they prevailed not because it was a whim on God's part but *because* 'they cried out' (prayed) in the middle of the battle'. How did they do that, we learn that it was because 'they trusted' in Him. In the middle of a battle, with real, live arrows, spears, chariots and horses and a lot of uproar and tumult we have a very good example of how God can hear above all that noise.

They cried out because of their need, not because God couldn't hear them – a quiet prayer in a noisy place is always heard.

If God can hear their prayer in the middle of a battle He can hear your prayer in a loud place, be it the middle of a supermarket or in the middle of any noisy place. So do try this regularly. Doing this sharpens our mind spiritually and we gain a proficiency of focus and concentration in situations that are noisy or uncomfortable when we need to pray in such circumstances in the future.

Prayer should always be *ready*. We need a readiness about us to talk with God – this is especially valuable when we are caught in a moment. And we know how to create that state of readiness:

> In happy moments praise God.
> In difficult moments seek God.
> In quiet moments worship God.
> In painful moments trust God.
> In every moment thank God.

Practising prayer in moments like these fortifies us to think through and more clearly articulate at all times. I think we are beginning to see the pattern that prayer in *different* circumstances strengthens us to be able to express ourselves well in *all* circumstances. Instead of stilted and muddled thoughts and expressions to God, we offer our inner self confidently because we are accustomed to sharing our thoughts with God.

This truly is a transformative skill. It's difficult to express adequately how much this will change your life. As we practise the exercise of talking with an Almighty Heavenly Father regularly, we discover that we also become consummate communicators with our fellow beings throughout life.

You will find yourself thinking more effectively of answers to questions from others; creating conversation with others more easily; dealing with confrontation more calmly; adding colour and illumination to your descriptions of situations. You'll have a new kind of confidence in almost any situation, learning that you not only have faith that God is there with you in all situations – but that you can communicate with an articulate assurance that you never imagined would be an amazing side-effect of talking with God!

If we can talk with God anytime, anywhere about anything – it empowers us with a skill for communicating with everyone.

One of the things I enjoy about prayer life that I would like to share with you is my 'prayer hour'. I won't tell you what hour mine is because you should set a prayer hour for yourself. I chose one that does not usually have a lot of activity around it, and is not connected with any other time, like the midday news I like to listen to.

This doesn't mean you need to pray for a whole hour – it just means that as the clock strikes that hour, we stop and remember prayer. We remember to associate a specific number on life's dial to prayer. You may choose 2 o'clock or 12 o'clock, whatever time is best for you. We automatically think about prayer at this time because we mentally link a formed habit, and habits are formed over several weeks, after which they're almost second nature.

So if every time you reach that chosen hour each day for the next few weeks and make a conscious effort to think about prayer and pray, you'll soon develop a life-long habit that's good for developing the spiritual mind.

Set aside time, or if in company excuse yourself for a moment. But every time that hour ticks over each day it is time to announce to yourself, 'This is the prayer hour' or 'I have reached the prayer hour.'

In our lives there are already a lot of *times* that mean something to us.
> We say, 'It's 9 o'clock! I should be at work – go, go, go, go, go.'
> Or, 'It's 5 o'clock, work is over. Stop, stop, stop.'
> Or another one, 'It's 7 o'clock, I should be on my way to Bible Class.'
> Or, have you heard this one? 'It's 10:30 and I'm running late for the memorial service!'

We can clearly see just how many times we have in our daily lives. So choose a time everyday where there is an hour to remind you that you have to be somewhere – and that somewhere is a special place where just you and God are for a moment. It is a place where just you and He share some precious one to one time. Where just your thoughts and God's will exist together. Decide a prayer hour for yourself.

I can't tell you that it will change your life more than any other practical idea here. But I can say that having a prayer hour certainly made a difference to my prayer life.

When prayer is difficult...

Whenever we find ourselves in circumstances against our will - talk about *His*. When prayer is difficult - just talk with God. This entire book is about talking with God because we are taking the whole concept of prayer to the next step – that is *living* it as well as just praying about it. If we let these moments lead us to prayer something very unexpected happens - we soon find ourselves talking with God all day.

That's what we want to achieve. More importantly, that's what God wants for us. That's what God really desires that we have – that is the *real* gift. Think about this phrase slowly and carefully:

> Prayer is the omnipresence God gifts to us!

Just as God is everywhere by His Spirit; we are everywhere by our prayers – because our prayer is to a God who is everywhere. Can you visualize this? Are you able to appreciate the incredible power of this principle? God wants you to!

If my friend in a far removed country is suffering trouble or turmoil, or is upset, ill, or worried – God is there. And God gives me the omnipresence of prayer. So I can pray to God and I am there with my friend through prayer. Isn't this an absolutely wonderful gift?!

The writer to the Hebrews says in chapter 4;

> "Since then we have a great high priest who has passed through the heavens, Jesus, the Son of God, let us hold fast our confession. For we do not have a high priest who is unable to sympathize with our weaknesses, but one who in every respect has been tempted as we are, yet without sin. Let us then with *confidence* draw near to the throne of grace, that we may receive mercy and find grace to help in time of need."

Jesus Christ had a life of prayer. He was God's Son and even though he received the Holy Spirit by God at his baptism – he *still* prayed. He had a great mind, a great friendship and a great relationship with his Father who was in heaven. We read that he went up to the tops of mountains and sometimes stayed there and prayed all night.

We read that just before miracles which he knew perfectly well that he could perform - he would pray. He would pray for people's forgiveness, he would pray for people's sins to leave them. He would pray for people to turn to God. He was the Son of God – and he prayed, and he prayed and he prayed *all* his life.

If it's good enough for him it's most certainly going to be good enough for us. If he did this as an example for us and talked as often as he did with his Father – then what's stopping us?

Jesus Christ lived a life of prayer and on top of that he paid an enormous price for our salvation. He opened the way for us to go through and so arrive at a deeper understanding and enter into a deeper relationship with our Heavenly Father. And he did it for us as well as himself. Jesus Christ paid the phone bill in advance my friends… and now the line is open.

Bless God in more of your life. Learn to share those hopes and those fears. Practise taking the elements of what you have and who you are and share them with God and I guarantee you will soon be sharing a more comprehensive, spiritually fulfilling relationship with your Heavenly Father. And that was the 'work' of Christ.

Thus we embrace this beautiful belief and we take it upon ourselves to grow spiritually and talk with God. We do this through our Lord Jesus Christ. We can take our praise, reflections and petitions to God through him.

A way has been made open. We must use it – and talk with God.

~ 2 ~
PRAISE
with
GOD

Voluntary wonder

So we made it to chapter two. In this section we are going to consider what we can experience by way of *Praise* with God. The psalmist says;

> "Let my prayer be set before thee as incense"

We really *do* have a very wonderful God. What He has done, and continues to do in our lives and His revelation of Himself to us, is something that we gradually and thankfully mature in comprehending. It's a blessing to be able to understand the great work of our Heavenly Father and at this point in our meditations we want to bring our minds to focus on this - and to be thankful.

The most sincere expression of thankfulness is something we call *praise*. There are probably numerous definitions of exactly what praise is - no doubt you can think of some yourself. For the moment, at least until we get our heads around some of the concepts surrounding this subject, let's take this one: *Praise is genuine recognition of someone as they are and for what they do; without any expectation of gain from the expression of that admiration.*

To be able to articulate our wonder at what He has done is a marvellous honour - be it by voice, prayer, song or any expression we have at our disposal. We investigate those deep waters of wonder – and swim in the currents of our Heavenly Father's blessings and stand, as the old Hymn says, 'in awesome wonder.'

A poet from the 17th century by the name of Edward Young said,

"Wonder is involuntary praise."

Playing a little on that phrase, we need to exercise in our lives a *fascination* with 'wonder'; because wonder is the beginning of praise. Praise should ultimately be spontaneous wonder.

This wonder is something that once put before us we pick up with both hands gently. We stare into it and through it and are filled with awe. We are just bursting with joy, curiosity and admiration – so we express this awe and wonder in genuine and various ways.

I want you to be able to take this idea and look at it this way because there is something very tangible, something eternal and natural about praise. In talking with God and by putting this fascinating element into our prayers, frequently and thoughtfully, we will have real and valuable praise for God.

Let's consider Psalm 141; which is where we read the phrase quoted earlier, "Let my prayer be set before thee as incense";

> "O LORD, I call upon you; hasten to me! Give ear to my voice when I call to you! Let my prayer be counted as incense before you, and the lifting up of my hands as the evening sacrifice! Set a guard, O LORD, over my mouth; keep watch over the door of my lips!"

The Psalmist portrays in these beautiful words, prayer as a type of incense. We all know what incense is, particularly how it was used in the time of the Tabernacle on the altar of incense as a great symbol of prayer. There was something *pleasing* about incense to God.

But more pleasing to Him was a simple illustration that we too can understand. Incense was an easy and relevant way for God to show to the people that this is what prayer should be. Prayer, like incense is:

- Directed upward
- Savoury, or pleasant
- Emanating from a source
- Laid out for all to see
- Produced with labour
- Offered with good intentions
- Long-lasting and memorable
- Repeatable
- Had a meaning that is relevant to other undertakings in life.

The act of offering incense made sense. It illustrated important spiritual principles intended to change the heart and make it wise in many aspects of worship and life.

There is something about the act of offering incense; giving a special gift in recognition places the giver in a position of reflecting back something to the Giver of All.

Praise must honour God

This should be an absolutely rock solid and vital foundation to our understanding of praise. If there is in prayer an effort to praise God that does not *honour* God – then it is not praise, and it is certainly not prayer.

The other day I was chatting with someone who was having a tough day, he had to explain in great detail all his problems. We had a couple of ideas about how to deal with the issues and how to approach things more positively – and even this was difficult.

Then he turned to me and said, 'Don't worry, on Sunday night we have a worship and praise service - and I'll be feeling better after that.'

I went away wondering how the worship service was going to benefit this person. Was it because *he* would get something out of it? True, there is an inbuilt and natural impulse within human nature that knows it needs to worship. But worship for the service of self is simply *not* worship. And it's *not* praise either!

Praise *must* honour God first – not the giver of the praise. If we offer or give praise and it doesn't benefit God it's just feel-good flattery, usually of self. Praise must always honour God for it to be accounted praise.

Here's a question. What if I came up to you and said, 'Listen friend, I really admire your good character and strong stand for things that matter, you are an inspiration to me' - you would probably feel a little, though entirely humble, glow of satisfaction – right?

But if you later overheard me saying to another person, 'My word, it made me feel so great to encourage that friend just now', you'd rightly do a double take, and wonder how genuine my praise of you actually was. My motive would be exposed and my seemingly good intention sullied.

Would we want to take that kind of praise to God? He does overhear things you know. In fact He knows the thoughts and intents of our heart before a word of praise escapes our lips!

I know - you or I would not do this kind of thing. But I know of at least one person who goes to a worship and praise service mostly for his *own* benefit! There are people out there who do that – don't fall into this confusion. Keep praise simple and of pure intentions.

God is (and has!) a very strong character – He doesn't 'need' our praise to feel good about Himself. But He does *desire* our praise to Him that forms or illuminates a reflection that He wants to see in us. It is our Heavenly Father's intention to fill the earth with His glory and that is how someone will feel better after a worship service. Praise must always glorify God.

As we have already discovered, prayer positions us in God's will. So when we praise God we want to do it on His terms. It's very difficult to position ourselves within God's will and offer Him meaningful praise if it doesn't honour Him.

If we receive benefit from praising God, then that should only ever be a side-effect, an unintended consequence of the praise that we give Him. An effect that places us and positions us in His will is:

- To be more like Him.
- To reflect His goodness.
- To reflect His awesome wonder.
- To reflect His purpose.
- To live His will.

Let's have a look at these key points because there are some practical and enduring concepts we can take forward.

Praise – being more like Him

On a clear night we can look up to the heavens and see the stars. The longer we look, the more stars we realize there actually are. Some of them we become familiar with, so when we look up we know which direction to face to find them again. Some are brighter than others but unless we are particularly perceptive they pretty much all look the same.

However, the advent of radio telescopes and deep space photographical equipment has made evident to our eyes that these stars are not all the same. Images of the stars and constellations are spectacular and an amazing kaleidoscope of colour is revealed.

Of course, we could elaborate further on the mind and the power that created such a display. But the point is that God is not a simple character – His character is multifaceted, more than our own characteristics are. Just as the stars appear to be all the same, so God may appear also; but on a closer inspection of His Word, He has revealed Himself a more colourful character than any we may meet again in our lives.

Being more like Him will be a natural product of our genuine praise. We look at an athlete or a performer achieving some great feat and in praising their attainment there is a little part of us that says, 'I wish I could *do that!*'

In the case of praising God our reaction is rather to *be like Him*. That is what He is looking for in us. When we praise Him and honour Him a little part of what it must be like to be what He is rubs off on us. Only a mind like His could possibly invent a concept such as praise that works like this.

Praise – reflecting His goodness

My grandmother has a long-standing joke when she calls me. She always asks me how I am – and I usually reply that I am good, and then she corrects me, "You're well – not good". And she's probably right.

I asked my niece the other day how her day at kindergarten was, to which she answered, "Good." It then took some further examination to discover what was *good* about it.

How do you define goodness? It can mean many states that are; well, OK, happy, fulfilled, correct, pleasant etc. The idea of the goodness of God comes from His own revelation of His character to Moses:

> "merciful and gracious, longsuffering, abounding in goodness and truth"

When I think of goodness, I think of something whole or wholesome, which may be a reasonable definition. But God's meaning of the attribute of goodness in His character is known as *loving kindness.*

So we ask ourselves the question when we praise the goodness of God; *can we honour and admire His loving kindness and not be moved to show loving kindness ourselves?* Sadly, in my case, the honest answer sometimes is "Yes." It's good for God to be good – but not for me. I'm working on that as you are probably doing so too.

One of the greatest compliments (praise) we can pay God is to do as He does. If He demonstrates loving kindness and we like that, it's highly probable that He likes us to be like Him in demonstrating the same characteristic. It's surprising how *well* we feel when we are *good*.

Praise – reflecting His awesome wonder

There's a well known photograph going around of a cat sitting in front of a mirror. His reflection however, is not that of a cat but of a lion.

Perhaps we are a little like that when we consider what aspects of God's awesome wonder we could possibly reflect. But God is the source and we are the reflection. When we praise God for what He has achieved in our tiny corner of His boundless universe, we cannot help but feel honoured to know, even in the most insignificant way, a little of Him.

The fact that He desires that we be His *children*, not merely His created beings, is a whole new awesome wonder in itself. In truth the more we understand this, and why, the more breath-taking we find it really is.

If you are like me, you probably find comprehending the vastness of space and the universe so unfathomable that it hurts your brain. It's just too big, too wide, too high and too deep. I just can't get my head around it all and in this mortal state I never will. It always makes me laugh to hear one of those poor evolutionists trying to explain so much as a *squillionth* part of it.

Equally, my brain also has trouble coming to grips with how blood circulates through the tiny body of an ant. And in that we have the key to this otherwise ridiculous dichotomy of the cosmos. How big is big – and how small is small?

If we can allow ourselves the failure to understand the end of the greatest and the conclusion of the smallest – then shouldn't there be a way that praising God for His awesome wonder that can be reflected in us? There is.

Just as God can fill space, so likewise He makes space for us to fill our minds with things greater and more important than simple animal existence. Our minds are small – His is great. Our time is limited – His is eternal.

As people who want to know more we have already acknowledged, in one small way, that we don't know it all. We have to leave what we don't know up to God. Our reflection therefore is not in creation but in *trust*. How much do we trust God? How much can we afford to? How much can we afford not to?

If we trust *entirely* we will have rendered to God an immeasurable praise that He can simply not achieve without us. It's only words, a small thing to write on a page – but the reward for trusting in God will be much more than this simple reflection now.

When Moses asked God what His Name was, God answered that it was, "I will be what I will be" - and His mirror never lies.

Praise – reflecting His purpose

What would living a spiritual life be like if we didn't have knowledge of God's purpose? Imagine going through life never knowing what could happen next – or what the past means. Take your Bible, hold it and imagine that instead of a single spine it had four of them all the way around and you could never open it. And no one else could either.

How would that make us feel? We'd have this wonderful book that we knew was sacred and important and it contained the very words, indeed the very mind of God. But it was shut, closed to us.

We wouldn't know of the stories, the examples, the prophecies, the advice and guidance, the promises or the hope contained in its pages. So, we'd just have to leave it on the shelf, perhaps in pride of place somewhere and sit around wondering what could possibly be inside. That would send me absolutely crazy – I'm far too curious to be able to bear not knowing what was in there, good or bad; I'd be desperate to know.

Then imagine, at some time in the future God performed His purpose and His plan and just *surprised us all*. His surprise would be truly wonderful if it was anything like what we know to be in the book that we *can* open. But He hadn't let us know, it was a big secret and He just wanted to see the look on our faces when we found out what He'd been hiding from us for all this time. It would most likely have the desired effect.

But how would we feel then? Perhaps if we'd known a little of what was inside the sealed book we could have done a better job at living a spiritually-minded life. If only God wasn't into playing the sealed-book-game then maybe we could have shared with Him our thoughts, feelings, excitement and wonder at what it contained. We could have told Him how absolutely fantastic His words and ideas were – and how precious His purpose really is and what it means for us to feel that way.

Well, as you've probably noticed, most Bibles we know of only have one spine that binds them, thank God! Really, thank God.

But how sad would it then be if we didn't open our Bibles and discover the words of hope and promise that He has made available to us *now*? There are some people who from one day to the next never bother to, never find the time to, or never find the curiosity to open the Book that God has prepared to declare His purpose. What are they waiting for? A big surprise perhaps?

Praising God for the wisdom and greatness of His purpose will always affect the giver of the praise in a small way. A way that grows day by day, year by year and forms an inner reservoir of spiritual thought that may always be tapped and shared with God.

Praise – living in the Will of God

I have a small dog. Some of you reading this may have even met *Zal* or heard of him before. His name means something like, 'a shadow' – and he follows me everywhere I go. In fact as I am writing this he is lying beside me, a little tired out from chasing his ball around.

Zal is a bright little chap. He is interested in *everything* and he learns very quickly. One day my brother and I estimated how many 'words' he knows. We gave-up after seventy (and that's not including names of individual people he recognizes!). But he's not human, despite what he may tell you - he is simply just a creature of many habits.

Every morning he comes back inside after his obligatory tour of the garden and expects his breakfast. He sits back at a polite distance from his food bowl and watches and waits. Eventually I get around to the most important meal of the day and over he comes.

It's the same routine for him; he sits up on his back legs, puts his little front paws together and waits for me to pray. He knows he cannot eat until prayer is said, so I pray for him, "Glory, glory, amen." Which in his little head is probably being interpreted as; *"Two, four, six, eight – got teeth, can't wait!"*

Now, in answer to the obvious question: No – I am not in the habit of praying with animals. On my part it is just a simple training mechanism to regulate his otherwise animal instinct to chow-down anything in sight without regard for whose food it is or what other dog's bowl he may come across.

Naturally, the consequence of such training is that when I'm having *my* breakfast it's not unusual to see a little dog praying in great earnest out of the corner of my eye - waiting for some rather hapless crumb to fall from his master's table!

But getting back to Zal's prayer, from a human perspective it *is* actually relevant to him. He doesn't know God and will never be able to comprehend who God is – much less communicate with Him as you and I can. But Zal *does* glorify God.

How? Zal performs the purpose God made him for. Be it only to entertain, amuse, comfort, guard, protect, exercise or teach me; the little dog *fulfils the purpose* God made him for – and therefore he demonstrates God's glory. The lily of the field, the sparrow on the breeze and the sands upon the seashore do exactly the same; all glorify their Creator because they *fulfil the purpose* He made them for.

As for us, we have a cerebral capacity to comprehend not only the purpose for which we were made but also the *will* behind the divine decision to make us. We know what God means when He says, "the earth will be filled with the knowledge of the glory of the LORD, as the waters cover the sea."

We glorify God when we put ourselves in that picture – and in prayer especially because we have the opportunity to praise Him for *living* as we were created for – to give God glory.

It is the glory of God that runs at the vanguard of His works – it's His will that gives energy to all His goodness and all His blessings. As Moses said, "Who among the gods is like you, O LORD? Who is like you - majestic in holiness, awesome in glory, working wonders?" What a great praise phrase!

Our challenge (our calling!) is to live a life *in* that will. Prayer is just a part of that and praise, just a part of prayer. Living in full confidence that God will perform His promises, and getting ourselves inside this will and going with it with Him, this *is* our calling.

As He has said:

> "Bring my sons from afar and my daughters from the ends of the earth - everyone who is called by my name, whom I created for my glory, whom I formed and made."

So there are a few thought-starters on the effects of a life in praise of God.

Tell God of your hope for a life with Him

When you praise God tell Him of your dreams. Tell Him of your hope for life filled with all the goodness that He offers. God wants that for you. He wants you to be as kind as He is, as loving as He is, as wise as He is – in some measure

In fact, if you believe His promises, He wants us to live as long as He does! That's why it's called the promise of *eternal* life.

As His children He genuinely wants these great blessings for us. So, praise to God that honours Him and positions us within His will for eternal life with Him fulfils what God desires for Himself and for us.

We can't earn salvation although it *is* conditional. Even so, imagine what it would be like to be the eternal, immortal God – and lose you or me because we don't want eternal life with Him. It's easy for us to get over the loss – because we'd be dead! But to God it's an eternal investment in memories. Which one will we wish on Him forever? This puts it in perspective doesn't it?

Tell God of your dreams for a life within His will. You will be a better son or daughter – and share a richer and more meaningful relationship with God.

One really important result of articulating our hope for eternal life *then* is that it positions us in His hope and will *now*. When this is our focus it affects our decisions and our life now. "We live, and move, and have our being" as if we were living the eternal existence we have yet to experience. The temptations, the one eye on worldly pursuits, the confusion of priorities, the sin, the worry, the stresses of this life are futile – we refuse to participate in what is not eternally-centred because we are already in our mind and hope living as if we already have the promise.

And we do already have the promise. If we believe the promise, and live as if it is part of the immutable will of the Almighty; just like Abraham, we are credited as stamped and *approved* by God of being worthy of such eternal life.

And that's a very good reason to praise God!

We shall be like Him

Psalm 115 is a wonderful example of praise in many ways. But the idea that stands out most in these words is that praising God actually makes us more like Him.

Speaking of heathen and their gods, the Psalmist explains,

> "Their idols are silver and gold, the work of human hands… Those that make them *become* like them; so do all who trust in them."

Most sensible people think worshipping rocks and metallic or wooden images is a bit crazy. Still, Buddhists revere their rotund statues, Muslims adore Mecca, and some religions even worship statues and icons of saints and so called relics.

And it's obvious that those adherents become like their idols, just as the Psalmist observed. They can be overtaken in a stultifying stupor of spiritual malaise and they, like the focus of their worship become stuck, stolid and incapable of fulfilling the purpose to which they themselves were made – to praise the only, eternal, living God.

> i·dol·a·try
> –noun, plural idolatries.
> 1. the religious worship of idols.
> 2. excessive or blind adoration, reverence, devotion, etc.

For others there are different forms of idolatry. An excessive or blind devotion to work, money, prestige, fame or a whole bunch of other obsessions I'm sure you can think of; are also destined to make those that worship them just like them.

There's probably someone who wants me to mention television worship too. I don't really want to because it's wheeled out too often as an example and it's an ever-changing medium dealt with by different people in different ways.

You do however, get the sense that some young people who spend far too much time with some fictional characters become like them – they even talk like them. For those who have that problem let me simply say, those people on the screen are *actors* for the most part. They don't really talk like that in real life and their real lives are a lot more boring than ours!

Choose the focus of your worship carefully because you are destined to *become* like it.

The really good news is that the rule is true for those who worship properly and who praise the One and Only Living God – they will become like Him.

That's why the Psalmist finished Psalm 115 with these words,

> "we will bless the LORD from this time forth and *evermore*. Praise the Lord".

In other words, not only will we *not* worship idols in case we also end up deaf, dumb and entirely senseless – but we *will* worship God because it is worth becoming like Him. That's eminently sensible!

Sleep on a prayer – awake with praise

Sometimes this is difficult for us to do. Sometimes we are too tired when we go to bed to pray to God, and sometimes we are all too reluctant to arise the following morning and get out of that nice warm place and live a life in praise.

Practise sleeping on a prayer and awaking with praise.

This is not just a novel little habit that may be fun to try for a while. It's actually fundamental to living with a sound mind. Most of us do this in part and some of us even do it with God in mind. But essentially we all go to sleep with something on our minds, a worry or a hope; and awake to find our place in the world again and approach the same with either a positive or negative mind-set.

If we sleep on a prayer and awake with praise, just like any other thoughts – we pick-up where we left off. The difference is that we control and take them to a spiritual level that is far more beneficial. Be thankful for the day that is before you and hopeful of the times you will share with your Heavenly Father.

From time to time, I find it difficult to pray before I go to sleep. But when I do, a more peaceful sleep follows. On a night of *unrest* it doesn't usually take me long to realize that I forgot to pray. However, when I do, things seem to go better than not praying at all. It's a reset for a spiritual mind.

It seems appropriate to thank God for His blessings throughout the day and conclude with the memory of Him and of what He has done as being the last thing on our mind before we finally fall asleep. It's not always the case that this is the last thing on my mind – my mind wanders off where it will but at least closing the day in prayer is in itself an 'amen' to the blessings and recognition of the day that has been.

Praying before sleep is actually the time we have to be most careful. Although I try to be sincere, if I am tired or concerned about something, I occasionally find my mind is on hold while my mouth is on automatic.

Sometimes I reach the end of the prayer and I can't even remember what I've said! Have you done that? When I realize what has just happened, that is precisely the time to go back and start again. God has not, in those circumstances been delighted by my prayer or my praise. We should remain mindful that our prayers are *heard* – don't pray with your mind on hold and your mouth on automatic.

We notice this problem sometimes in communal prayers. Whether they are at a memorial service or at a Bible class, someone is praying and you think, 'That brother always uses the same phrases and he always says the same thing.' It's very easy to do.

The next time *you* pray for your lunch or your evening meal, take note of the words you use. Do they roll dispassionately off your tongue in a simple formula you use time after time? Is that the kind of prayer that you would like to receive? Is there praise within it that positions you in the will of God – *actually* thankful for and hopeful of what you receive?

To be committed to our own lives in prayer we need to be mindful of what we say. We know we need to be careful of what we say to each other – how much more *thoughtful* should we be about what we say to an ever loving Heavenly Father?

How much effort should we put in to make both our moments awake and asleep part of our daily endeavour to live *always* with Him? My guess would be whatever it takes. The benefits are immediate – the rewards are eternal.

Always be grateful and thankful

When you can, try praying with a hymn book or a praise book. If you can make the time and open your hymn book you put yourself in another's position and pray their prayer. When we do this we are offering a praise that positions us within the will of God and pleases God because we are trying to be more like him. We are drawing closer to Him by expressing words that are not necessarily our own - we are *developing* our minds beyond our own experiences.

When we look back on our life and reflect on where we were when we learnt particular words, we form a certain pattern in our minds that associates memory. Our minds are basically squishy flesh through which chemicals and electrical impulses pass. Each time these *associate* they form an automatic *connection*, a recognizable pattern. The next time we see something similar it traces the same path through our brain following the same connection, testing the association.

When we are continuously putting in new information, we are constantly developing a broader variety of these memory paths within our minds. If we only put in good thoughts (which is very difficult to do!), and spiritual thoughts all day - our mind will become accustomed to tracing just spiritual paths within our mind. Because the human experience is not altogether good in reality, we depend on good patterns, good connections to help us cope or deal with the negative, less desirable occasions.

Pray with a hymn book or song book and you create healthy new paths. If you only had cereal for breakfast, lunch and dinner the experience would be familiar but also a little bland and boring. If you suddenly had that pattern broken with a big serve of lemon meringue pie you can imagine your taste buds would go crazy.

On a less dramatic scale, different (healthy!) sources and influences enrich our spiritual mind and build a store of fresh resources to keep our prayers and communication vibrant and lively. You'll need this in your kit if you are to always be grateful and thankful.

Pray with your Bible open – get some more information in; read just two verses and pray about them. Doing something different like this on a regular, daily basis develops a *creative*, flexible and willing spiritual mind. The more we do this, the more we will find ourselves able to discover God in all aspects of our life and of course express our appreciation in prayer and praise.

Being grateful or thankful is not something we talk about much but I think we should. Are we thankful for our job – or do we think the boss is incredibly fortunate to have us working for him? Note: This question still applies to you if you work for yourself! Are we grateful for our friends and family – or do we wonder what on earth they would do without us? You get what I mean.

I think I should tell you a story about being grateful, in which you can see yourself in the same spiritual lesson. The events are easily transferred as metaphors for your life too.

Many years ago, as a little boy, my parents and some family friends hired a house boat and went for a week of river cruising. This house boat had a large paddle-wheel at the rear which propelled the vessel along.

In a moment of adventure, a couple of friends decided that we would take the little launch boat, tie it to the big boat, jump in and get towed by the big house-boat.

This was fun for a while but the novelty wore off soon enough. To return to the big boat required pulling on the rope to get closer to the big boat. In hindsight someone should have realized that doing this would bring the little launch into serious trouble in the form of some rather insurmountable waves thrown up by the paddle-wheel on the boat we were trying to re-board.

The waves came up and the launch went down - to the bottom. The three of us were in the big river, the house-boat steaming off into the distance – and I couldn't swim.

The little experience I'd had with water didn't include big rivers and certainly didn't include being in a large body of flowing water without a life-jacket. To make this story shorter, fortunately someone on board the paddle-boat *happened* to be walking around the back, spotted us and yelled for the boat to be turned around – *I was grateful*. My friend in the water helped me – *I was grateful*. Finally back on board someone wrapped a blanket around my frightened, shivering little body – *I was grateful*.

The experience could have made me terrified of going near water ever again. Instead it made me determined not only to learn to swim but to become a strong swimmer – *I was grateful*.

A couple of years later we were visiting a busy public pool (ironically just a few miles from that river!) with a couple of other kids all under the supervision of my mother. Not wanting to leave the younger ones unattended she sent me to the vehicle to get the sunscreen someone had forgotten.

When I walked back in the gate my mother was standing on the other end of the pool screaming her head off. I noticed it straight away, the volume and waving her arms about did it I think. She was trying to get someone, anyone, to help a lady who had strayed out of her depth and was in serious trouble. Everyone was standing around watching, not willing or able to do anything. In about the same time it took me to discover what she was actually screaming about, she spotted me in the distance and (unbelievably) increased her volume even further with the urgent demand that *I* do something.

It was a big pool. I was only a little chap. But I knew what it felt like to be out of my depth and have someone help me Perhaps it was this, together with a dose of adrenalin and not a little exasperation at all the *big* people just standing around doing nothing that made me act. Immediately, I dived into the pool and swam my little heart out until I reached the lady. Reaching down I heaved until she came up, put my hand under her chin and swam as hard as I could with my free arm to the pool edge.

She took a while to recover as she was very shaken – but she was grateful. And I know what that feels like.

God is in the life-saving business big-time! And for that we should be grateful – *always*.

Praise has a wider audience

If you've got your Bible with you, turn to Hebrews chapter 13. Hebrews 13 is one of my favourite chapters because it is all about *communication*. It's all about relating to God and each other. It's a great chapter. We read there;

> "By him [Jesus Christ] therefore let us offer the sacrifice of praise to God continually, that is, the fruit of our lips giving thanks to his name. But to do good and to communicate forget not: for with such sacrifices *God is well pleased.*"

Notice here the conditions that the Apostle Paul is laying down. Firstly he says, "let us offer the *sacrifice* of praise" – he doesn't call it the gift of praise. It's not this kind of surplus thing that we have - Paul calls praise *a sacrifice*. Secondly, he says, to offer praise "continually".

And in the next verse he says,

> "Do not neglect to *do good* and to *share*."

'Share' means to *communicate*. Paul is comparing what he said in verse 16 to what he said in verse 15. In verse 15, praise should be a *sacrifice* and a *continuous* one; and in the next verse he tells us not to forget our actions – in other words, don't forget to live the *same way* that you praise! Remember to talk about with others what we talk about with God. These are the sacrifices that God is *pleased with*.

And this is what it means to be thankful: To express gratitude both in word and in action to God and to others.

In 1 Chronicles 16 David is bringing the Ark of the Tabernacle into Jerusalem:

> "And they brought in the ark of God and set it inside the tent that David had pitched for it, and they offered burnt offerings and peace offerings before God. And when David had finished offering the burnt offerings and the peace offerings, he blessed the people in the name of the LORD."

What David is doing here is *communicating* the praise of God to the other people present. Then David tells the people to *reciprocate*. He encourages them to do the same thing and he says,

> "Oh give thanks to the LORD; call upon his name; make known his deeds among the peoples."

David wants everyone to reflect this praise,

> "Oh give thanks to the LORD, for he is good; for his steadfast love endures forever! Say also: "Save us, O God of our salvation, and gather and deliver us from among

the nations, that *we may give thanks to your holy name, and glory in your praise*... to give thanks to the LORD, for his steadfast love endures forever."

Making a sacrifice in praise, *giving of ourselves continually* is the first stage. Living it and doing good, or *making good* on our expressed values is the second stage. Telling or showing others and *encouraging* them to do likewise is the third stage. An even wider audience will *notice* this and that is the fourth stage.

Now it may not always work out in that order. But as far as we are concerned, that is as far as we are able to set our priorities and consequently our influence. This is how praise to a wider should unfold.

It reminds me of Daniel, who followed this way of life to the letter.

First, he *sacrificed* himself in praise to God. Secondly, he *continually* made a habit of praying to God, three times a day we read. Thirdly, others saw his devotion; they even tried to use it against him. Fourthly, he ended up in the lion's den – was delivered by God; and now millions of people have been talking about Daniel and his sacrifice of praise for around 2,400 years. How's that for an example of praise to God reaching a wider audience?!

Honour God's name

Fundamental to our praise should be honour of His name. Learn God's name, understand it well – and show God's name to others. In doing so we make praise evident, we give mere thoughts life. We make them *alive*.

In all our prayers and in all our praise remember God as our Father. This is something that we can really relate to, isn't it?

In the Epistles of John, even though they are short, it is worth noting that John uses the term 'Father' 17 times in just a few pages! Remember this when you are reading through the Epistles of John. It's an interesting exercise to underline each occasion in a coloured pencil. He says in one chapter;

> "See what kind of love the Father has given to us, that we should be called children of God; and so we *are*. The reason why the world does not know us is that it did not know him. Beloved, we are God's children *now*, and what we will be has not yet appeared; but we know that when he appears [Jesus Christ] we shall be like him, because we shall see him as he is. And everyone who thus hopes in him purifies himself as he is pure."

So, in praising God we actually purify our minds and become more like God, more like our Heavenly Father – that's real praise. This honours Him.

We admire our Heavenly Father for *who He is* and *what He has done*. A friend of mine was recently in Israel and sent a little saying that he found in their hotel room. It simply said;

> 'Good morning, this is God. Today I shall be dealing with all your problems. I shall not need your help. Have a good day.'

God really does so much for us. He doesn't *need* us. He doesn't *need* our praise. But our Heavenly Father *wants* us, and He *wants* our praise.

We can make time to look at the prayers of Jesus. They are a great inspiration and guidance. Of course, we have the Lord's Prayer, which we know well. It's a good example of praise, reflection and petition. It's a very good example of talking with God. But go through the rest of the prayers in Christ's life sometime. Maybe put aside your daily readings for one day if you don't have time to do both and spend a few moments looking at these prayers.

Christ's life and example is inspirational and most relevant to us. He is not God, he is God's Son – but his life was so in tune with God's Word, God's thoughts, God's ideals, God's desire and he was so obedient to all that God *is*. In his life he was living the God life. Not God's life but a God-like life.

Those who first knew Christ, who saw and heard him, were seeing and hearing the closest thoughts, ideals and actions of God Himself. Christ was fulfilling the name of God in his own life. The *I will be* (Yah) was being lived out in Christ – word and deed.

There are many ways to honour God's name. It's good to become familiar with all the ways in which we can give God true praise, true honour; but living a God life (or Godly life) is where all the aspects of praise meet in one comprehensive expression of pure honour. We show reverential esteem for the purpose and being of He who has the Name '*I will be who I will be*' (Yahweh). Wanting to *be* like God and seeking to attain that spiritual character isn't just a compliment to God but also a hand-in-hand fulfillment of the very purpose of God – and this pleases God very much.

Just as Paul and the disciples addressed the Thessalonians;

> "we urge and exhort you in the Lord Jesus that you should abound more and more, just as you received from us how you ought to walk [literally, *to make progress*] and to please God."

Abounding (*exceeding the measure*, as this means) more and more is just how God lives, how He thinks, how He gives (and forgives!) – these are all at the core of living a God-life. *Being* is doing and doing *is* praise.

For those who honour God's name and care about a deeper relationship with Him, it's unlikely that they will choose to dishonour His name.

Sometimes there are elements of communication that creep into our communities that seem innocuous at first but really end up to our harm. You know the really bad words, the terrible blasphemous ones that assault the ears. But there are other examples too.

One that is particularly irritating is the increasing use of the abbreviation, 'OMG' – which is used a lot on more recent forms of technology. OMG means 'Oh my God', and quite how it ends up in some communication is still a total a mystery!

Is OMG blasphemy? No, I don't think we can put it in that class of words or phrases. Does its use honour God? Most of the time the answer is definitely 'No'. However, we can in fact use the prevalence of this phrase to honour God.

Some years ago I used to give a lift to an old Italian brother from his home to take him to Sunday Assembly – and he used this phrase all the time. He would be describing some catastrophe of the week, something akin to burning the toast or stubbing his toe, and would in the telling thereof often exclaim, 'Oh mio Dio!'

At first it bothered me a little until I came to realize that this dear old brother wasn't telling me, 'Oh my God' – he was telling God, 'Oh my God'. The story was for me but the exclamation was for God. In fact, this brother, when you got to know him, spent most of his life talking to God – he told God everything!

Have I used this phrase? Yes, I do use it occasionally - generally in times of great excitement or terrible distress. It's not my habit to use the phrase if I spill my cup of tea, but I do remember saying 'Oh my God' as I watched the second airplane crash in to the World Trade Centre live on TV. Witnessing the sudden and catastrophic loss of life moved one to the instantaneous prayer of just three words when no more words could be found.

So, let's take something from this and make a general rule. If the phrase is used *to* God it's honouring Him – if it's used to someone else, it's probably not. Let's all make a promise to only praise with the phrase.

Finally, I find it a really great opportunity to preach the Gospel! If someone says in conversation, 'Oh my God' I say, 'I'm so glad you mentioned God, I didn't know you were a believer. You know I was thinking about God earlier today and really wanted to ask someone…'

Investing in praise

In your praise, pray with poetry, pray with song and even experiment with prayer in rhyme. Each time we do something different like this we are making an *investment* in our expression to God. If a child comes to the parent and says, 'Mummy, I love you' or 'Daddy, I love you' – one is moved by the child's thoughts and feelings. We say they are sincere, guileless; their praise is a beautiful expression of that.

But if the child were to draw a picture of himself and his mother and father, and his brothers and sisters, what would the effect then be? If he were to create a picture of *togetherness* that raised this child's love in praise to his parents and outwardly exhibited those feelings that said that he appreciated what his parents had done for him then that child has made an additional *effort* – an additional 'investment' in their relationship.

Therefore the picture goes straight to the refrigerator door. A parent feels much more moved by the child's 'investment' in his thoughts and feelings toward his loved and loving parents. The parent actually thinks just as much of the *time* the child spent making the artwork than of the finished design itself.

How does our Heavenly Father feel about our efforts, our commitment, our investment in expressing praise and thanksgiving to Him? Does it measure up to that of a 3 or 4 year old? If not, we've some great examples right there in our lives!

There are plenty of Scriptural examples of investing in praise. One that springs to mind is when David brought that Ark of the Covenant to Jerusalem. Just imagine being there on the sidelines of that great procession, all the people, musical instruments, the choreographed pageantry, sacrifices and even the after-party supper including bread, meat and wine – all for the praise of God.

When you think about it, there was really no need for all the fuss. The whole thing could have just as easily been carried out on a low-key, rather mundane administrative level. Perhaps there was some advisor who recommended the whole thing be done at night – you know, like road works – so as not to cause unnecessary traffic jams on Jerusalem's narrow streets.

But David wouldn't have any of that, no way; he was going to invest the maximum effort in praising God and to bring the people along with him. He invested in the moment and used it to praise God.

If a 4 year old child and one of the greatest kings that ever lived both know how to invest in praise – surely you and I fall somewhere in between and can make an investment commensurate with our faith and desire to further the will of our Heavenly Father.

How? Well, I have to leave that to your discretion because you know how the situations and opportunities are going to pan-out for your life and more importantly what you can invest.

But as a guide, try this method: Parables!

Have you ever thought about how many of the Parables spoken by Jesus are about investment? In fact, a significant 63% of his parables *feature* money or valuable goods in their narrative (and this figure doesn't even include those that put a price on an investment in 'time'). For those seeking an eternal treasure, we could rightly say that Jesus was the greatest investment advisor that has ever lived!

If it's not money, goods or crops in a parable it's something else *tangible* that Christ uses to illustrate spiritual virtue. That's a good indication to us that investing in praise requires something tangible, at least something we can in some way measure the spiritual health of our prayer resources.

For some it's something simple like an investment of time in writing a prayer journal. For one sister who's into scrapbooking it's a project that reflects her interest and abilities. For the brother who's into gardening it is planting fruit trees that have Scriptural or spiritual significance that he can reflect on as God makes them grow. I'm deliberately trying to curb my enthusiasm for giving you a lot of examples because we all have a different interest or ability we can use!

Remember though, the idea is to *invest* in praise – not invest in goods, or for that matter attempt to invest in God. We will never be in a place where the little we give equals the life and blessings He has given us. It's not giving to a cause or a spiritual savings fund – instead it's about *investing in a relationship* like no other.

Pray with confident humility

Praise that is neither confident nor at the same time humble is without direction – it's uncertain of its foundation and vague about its destination. Learn to build into your praise to God confidence in what He can do and the humility to recognize what He has already done for you. That is praise.

There's an old theological nonsense question that goes something like this, 'Can an All-powerful God create a stone so heavy that He cannot lift it?' The semantics of the question are put so that either way God is unable to do something, and therefore He's not *all*-powerful. It is known as the 'omnipotence paradox.'

Some philosophers have wasted a great deal of time debating this paradox. From where I stand, the answer to the question is simple – 'No, he cannot'. Why? Because the question is argued from a human level and doesn't take into account the word or the nature of God. Both are a level or two beyond whether He can lift something or not.

The Word of God says, God cannot be tempted, God cannot sin and God cannot die. Here are at least three examples of things that God cannot do. These make Him more, not less powerful because He cannot do them. Therefore we are the more confident and humbled by such knowledge.

Prayer moves the hand that moves the world. Understand what our Heavenly Father has done and what He will do – thank Him for letting us speak with Him about that. And together we remain with Him in confident humility.

We are confident because He will always do what is *right* for us, not because He will do whatever we ask Him. He's far too wise a Father to trust us to make all the right decisions for ourselves. Thus for that quality of care we truly praise *His* judgement.

Praise God for difficult problems. This is a real challenge that builds the character that He is looking for in each and every one of us. I know some of you may have some very challenging problems. I don't know how I would deal with some of them; likewiseI have some challenges in my life that I'm sure you would find difficult to deal with! But our Heavenly Father is with us throughout all of them. It takes character, it takes practice, it takes humility and it takes a great deal of confidence to be able to thank God for difficult problems.

Nancy Spelberg wrote,

> 'LORD I crawled across the barrenness to you with my empty cup, uncertain in asking for any drop of

refreshment. If I'd only known you better, I'd have come running with a bucket.'

Thank God for difficulties in your life. Grow in the confidence that you can actually praise God for them and that they will not ruin your confidence – but will instead *create* and inspire confidence.

Praise God for interesting opportunities. So many of us see so many exciting things ahead of us in our lives or there is something we want to do. Perhaps you are starting a new job, or a new position, or you have a change of direction in your life – thank God for those new opportunities. Ask Him specifically that those opportunities will allow you to praise Him more. This is because praising God can really take in all circumstances of our life. In living a life of prayer *continually* we acknowledge God in *all* aspects of our life.

One of my favourite prayers is called 'The Fisherman's Prayer'. I find it somewhat cute but it reminds me that we need God for our *entire* life and that we should always remember that He is there and praise Him. For me this prayer expresses the kind of confidence and humility we need and the simplicity of an entire life of prayer. The Fisherman's Prayer goes like this;

> God grant that I may live to fish until my dying day,
> And when my final cast I've made and life has slipped away,
> I pray that God's great landing net may catch me in its sweep
> And that in His mercy God will judge me...
> Big enough to keep.

Get to the point

Some prayers are long and meaningless. Hopefully, those kind of prayers don't come from us. You've probably heard the saying that some prayers need to be cut short at both ends and set on fire in the middle!

Jesus' instruction on prayer is helpful. He speaks about the motivation of prayer, types of prayer, the practice of prayer and even where to pray at different times. There were times when he obviously had a lot of matters to discuss with his Father "and spent the night praying to God."

But there were many more times when he was specific in his praise of, reflection on and petition to his Father. Here are three quick, to the point examples:

Praise – "Father, glorify thy name".
Reflection – "Your kingdom come, your will be done, on earth as it is in heaven."
Petition – "Father, forgive them, for they do not know what they are doing."

There was always something for the Son of God to communicate about with his Father in his personal life and in his ministry. We can imagine he spent many hours in prayer – but he also had times when his prayers were short and to the point.

This is demonstrated in the parable he told of the Priest with his long, rambling, self-important prayer juxtaposed with that of the tax-collector who simply entreated, "God, have mercy on me, a sinner."

When I was a child at Sunday school, I remember sitting through the memorial service with my friends. Why our parents ever trusted us alone I still don't really know. We didn't get into too much trouble but we used to sit together and the service just seemed so long some Sundays, we just couldn't wait to stand up for something or have the meeting over so we could get outside and play. Hey, I'm being honest here.

But as the service drew to a close it would always be of paramount interest to us as to which brother was going to close with prayer – and it was always a surprise because we never knew who the chairman had asked to do this. There were two brothers that we used to dread. I think the groan from our pew was almost audible if either of these two came up.

It seemed that it was easier to sit through an hour-long sermon than it was to stand for a fifteen minute prayer! And looking back at it now it's actually funny to think how much effort we put into worrying if one of those two names came up.

I can still see these two brothers in my mind now. One used to pray for quantity – not a single word he emitted remains in my memory to this day.

The other brother also used to pray for a long time – but when I reflect on his prayers now I realize that his prayers were not full of asking God for this or that. A very large part of his prayer was mainly devoted just to praising God. And each sentence got to the point without superfluous embellishments of speech-making. He just had a lot of things to praise God for.

Not many people pray like that anymore. Perhaps they 'suffered' the same as I did as a child. I'd not like to think that the next generation thinks that a short prayer is a good prayer no matter what is said.

The point is get to the point and make a large proportion of time in praising God *meaningful*.

The four building blocks of praise

Let's have a look briefly at Psalm 150, just to give a couple of final pointers on prayer and praise to take with us. As you read through this very short Psalm, you'll recognize some of these phrases very well!

> "Praise the Lord. Praise God in his sanctuary; praise him in his mighty heavens.
> Praise him for his acts of power; praise him for his surpassing greatness.
> Praise him with the sounding of the trumpet, praise him with the harp and lyre, praise him with timbrel and dancing, praise him with the strings and pipe, praise him with the clash of cymbals, praise him with resounding cymbals.
> Let everything that has breath praise the Lord.
> Praise the Lord."

Remember we looked at Elijah - God asked Elijah when he was in the cave, "Elijah, what are you doing *here*?" Just a small thing in Scripture, but I like these little things; God didn't ask him, "Elijah, what are you doing *there*?" He said *here* not *there*.

Psalm 150 starts off the same way. Praise God where He is. It's a big point actually because if He's not *in* our life much, maybe we are praying to God *there* instead of *here*.

- Praise God where He is

- Praise God for what He does

- Praise God with anything you have

- Praise God with what you have been given

These are the four building blocks of effective praise of God. The foundation, as we discovered earlier, is that praise must honour God. Now we have these four little building blocks that go on top of that foundation as we start to build-up our prayer life.

Where He Is	What He does	With what you have	With what is given
Praise must honour God			

Psalm 150 is our reminder chapter for this!

> "Praise the LORD! Praise God in his sanctuary; praise him in his mighty heavens!"

That's praising God *where He is!*

> "Praise him for his mighty deeds; praise him according to his excellent greatness!"

That's praising God *for what He does!*

> "Praise him with trumpet sound; praise him with lute and harp!
> Praise him with tambourine and dance; praise him with strings and pipe!
> Praise him with sounding cymbals; praise him with loud clashing cymbals!"

That's praising God *with anything you have!*

> "Let everything that has breath praise the LORD! Praise the LORD!"

That is praising God *with what you have been given!*

When God created Adam back in the garden of Eden He breathed into his nostrils the breath of life. If we are using the breath of life within us to praise God then we are certainly praising God with what we too have been given.

We must remember in our praise that it must honour God. And those four little building blocks can then be put on top of that basis:

Praise God where He is…
Praise God for what he does…
Praise God with anything you have…
Praise God with what you have been given.

Praise with God is to live a life of prayer - ***full of wonder!***

~ 3 ~
REFLECTION
with
GOD

Waking moments

Here we are at chapter 3 and we continue together in prayer and hope. This chapter on 'Reflection with God' is designed to lead us to a deeper understanding in prayer in approaching our Heavenly Father, how we relate to Him as a Father, how we share with Him our thoughts and also as to who He is to us and who we are to Him.

In Psalm 5 we read these words;

> "O LORD, in the morning you hear my voice."

In the last chapter where we discussed praise we used the phrase, 'Sleep on a prayer, and arise in praise.' As an extension to that we have the day before us during which we want to share with God as many of our waking moments as we can.

The truth is that we do share them with Him whether we recognize it or not. He is everywhere, He knows our thoughts and He knows our actions and our deeds. Becoming closer to God through prayer in a spiritual relationship with Him is about acknowledging this and being mindful of this for as much of our day as possible.

Hence this is where we reflect on the will, on the purpose, on the character and on the blessings of our Heavenly Father. In prayerful reflection with God, we actually endeavour to put between God and ourselves a spiritual and eternal bridge that links us in unity and in purpose.

To reflect can mean several things; you will understand by meditation on the word reflection or the in act 'to reflect', that several things can happen during reflection. It's not just about a simple mirroring, although that is still an element of what we need to do. The word *reflect* means;

- To *throw or cast back* light or heat or sound
- To *show an image* of something.
- To *have something* as a source or a cause.
- To *think deeply* in an exploratory manner.
- To *bring something to be* such as credit or discredit.

It's not the case that one of these definitions specifically defines how we should reflect with God. As we will discover, they are all equally important definitions. Each can be used as touchstones and reminders to create a vibrant, as well as extensive understanding of reflecting with God. So we'll look at each of them further:

Reflect: To *throw or cast back* something

We are able to ***throw back*** in a number of ways. As a kid I often played the simple school yard or back yard game of 'kick-to-kick' with my brothers or friends. This is about as simple a game as possible; it involved two or more people standing a reasonable distance apart and then kicking and catching a ball. It wasn't a game that anyone really won or lost. In fact, if you tried to win the other party would leave and you'd have no one to play with.

The skill was in kicking the ball so close to the other person (or a big bunch of boisterous boys) at the opposite end so that they *can* catch it. It was no fun kicking the ball way over their heads or too short, nor was it very interesting to kick it in another direction – because there would be no one to kick it back to you.

And in the game, if the level of skill at either end was different you simply changed the distance. I mean, there was no point going back sixty feet if your little brother could only kick it as far as six feet - and even that in a dubious direction.

I could give you an example about *throwing back* as a reflection in a mirror, or sound bouncing as it does in an echo; but I think this game describes the relationship with God better. He's a loving, caring and definitely *active* Father who wants to share His skill in things spiritual with us.

Throwing back as a reflection with God is not a game that is scored, not in its minutiae anyway. God knows any delivery from Him can easily sail far over our heads. However, we know in which direction we should be directing our attempts at spiritual reflection. And while God is always keen to see our level of proficiency improve - He is also merciful in reducing the gap when our ambition to participate exceeds our ability to accomplish.

It's not a matter of reducing our understanding of reflecting with God to a simple game of catch. That's just a simplification to get us started, a child-like parable to illustrate the principle that this reflection isn't static like standing in front of a mirror – instead it is participatory, lively and dynamic.

It's the kind of reflection that *does*. God is faithful - therefore I will be faithful. God is merciful - therefore I will show mercy. God has blessed me - therefore in reflecting on His blessings I too will be generous to a fault in my life. We can take any other value or virtue in the spiritual arsenal and apply ourselves to reflecting it also.

Reflect: To *show an image* of something

We are able to reflect on how our *image is relative to His*. I think it's probably safe to say that anyone who has seriously prayed to God has at one time or another, even if just in passing, wondered what the God they are praying to 'looks' like. And I don't think it's a coincidence that God has given us this concept of *image*.

Right back in the beginning, "God created mankind in his own image, in the image of God he created them; male and female he created them." Now there was actually a reason for this and in it we have a really big clue as to why image matters!

The reason is: "so that they may rule over the fish in the sea and the birds in the sky, over the livestock and all the wild animals, and over all the creatures that move along the ground." Now how does that make sense? A giraffe's image is bigger than ours, a shark's more fearsome, a cheetah's more fleet, a horse's more powerful and dozens of other animals are more physically suited to the attributes of 'rule' than ours. What sets us apart from the rest of the animal kingdom is that only humans have a cognitive ability to *reason* in terms of image.

Sure lions can recognize other lions and there's no chance a dog is going to start dating a cat - visual clues are obviously an important part of instinct and animal behavior. But not in a way that is nuanced, that can be reasoned or over which they have moral control.

Let me give you an example based on the very concept of image itself. I look at myself in a mirror at least twice a day. Once I get over the fright then I'm there with it, "OK, that's me." Animals do this rarely.

So you and I have a pretty good grasp of what we look like, right? Well, not always... Here's where it gets messy! For instance, you were at a picnic yesterday where someone took a photo of you just chilling out with your friends. You were not intoxicated, you had not done anything that would noticeably change your looks (like shave half your head or something equally crazy), you were not standing in or on anything dangerous – you were just being the most normal version of you, much like the one in the mirror. Yet when they show you the photo the next day you say, "Yikes, that looks nothing like me!"

And, YES! I just caught you *reflecting*.

Because we have this innate ability to recognize, reason, manipulate, deny, judge and record image mentally we are more like God than any other creature and He designed this deliberately.

Notice while we're on the subject those words, "in the image of God he created them; male and female he created them." God is male but He can still create a woman in His image because it's not the physical gender image that is being referred to but the ability to comprehend image just like God does.

And yes, a nod to fellow students of the Word who will quickly remind me that the word God is *Elohim* (mighty ones) in the original Hebrew. The mighty ones were outworking Almighty God's will but we still have to answer the question as to where they got their perception of image from! Recognition of image is paramount to human comprehension of value.

This is why Paul says of Christ in his letter to the Philippians, "being found in appearance as a man, he humbled himself by becoming obedient to death— even death on a cross!"

Jesus Christ couldn't change his physical image just by being humble or obedient. He was the same Jesus as his family and disciples would recognize right up to hanging on the cross as he passed from a state of life to death. Furthermore they recognized him after his death, in his immortality, *because* he still had the marks of the cruel nails in his hands.

The fact that we have this complex understanding of image is just the gift that God has given us to distinguish one image of ourselves from another, which takes us on to reflecting together with God.

Christ did – "Who being the brightness of his glory, and the express image of his person, and upholding all things by the word of his power, when he had by himself purged our sins, sat down on the right hand of the Majesty on high."

It is what Christ *did* (because he had reflected on doing it) that made him in this type of image with God. Not that God and Jesus now have the exact same looks; for the wordsmiths – the phrase 'the express image' is *one* word in the Greek text; *character*!

And it is this character reflection of the image of God that Paul speaks of us having *now*, when he writes:

> "put on the new self, which is being renewed in knowledge in the **image** of its Creator. Here there is no Gentile or Jew, circumcised or uncircumcised, barbarian, Scythian, slave or free, but Christ is all, and is in all. Therefore, as God's chosen people, holy and dearly loved, clothe yourselves with compassion, kindness, humility, gentleness and patience. Bear with each other and forgive one another if any of you has a grievance against someone. Forgive as the Lord forgave you. And over all these virtues put on love, which binds them all together in perfect unity."

Reflect: To *have something* as a source or a cause

While we can explain this in a number of ways, I think the easiest way is to lift a passage straight out of Scripture:

> "For just as through the disobedience of the one man the many were made sinners, so also through the obedience of the one man the many will be made righteous."

Paul hits the nail right on the head in this verse; we have both *source* and *cause* - the source of sin and the righteous cause that *short-circuits* it. It is highly probable that you have already done quite a lot of this kind of reflection in your prayers; now we are just defining it.

It's probably playing with tintacks but there are multiple meanings in English for the word *cause* as well – there's the *be-cause* and the *right-cause*: i.e. The cause of the corruption was greed, therefore the people took-up the cause for transparency in governance.

There's plenty of room in reflecting on both; the cause *of* and the cause *for*. We are able to understand the causes and sources of our existence, our state of (well)being, our feelings, our issues, our challenges and anything else in our lives. Having time to reflect on them with a prayerful mind is liberating and defines our direction forward in whatever human-nature challenged state we find ourselves, with the ongoing desire to be more like our High Priest and great example, Jesus Christ.

Reflect: To *think deeply* in an exploratory manner

We are able and very much encouraged to *think more deeply* on our spiritual life. To some degree we are sharing that journey a little right now.

To 'meditate' these days often means that the participant is trying to 'empty his head'. If this practice is for some form of relaxation it is sometimes physically or emotionally healthy to do so – but never for spiritual reasons.

In fact, some western, would-be-followers of eastern religions claim that for spiritual reasons they practise this for some kind of spiritual attainment. However, in reality even *real* Buddhists and Taoists don't attempt this in their observances; they go more along the line of emptying the head of wants and desires (not thoughts!), in readiness to receive a divine attainment of some kind. So even they don't want the kind of meditation that approaches nihilism.[1]

And there is of course the wisdom of Christ in the parable of the unclean spirit:

> "When an evil [unclean] spirit comes out of a man, it goes through arid places seeking rest and does not find it. Then it says, 'I will return to the house I left.' When it arrives, it finds the house unoccupied, swept clean and put in order. Then it goes and takes with it seven other spirits more wicked than itself, and they go in and live there. And the final condition of that man is worse than the first."

Taking a popular mythology of the day, Jesus used this parable to warn against the psychological danger of having an empty mind.

---

[1] Nihilism, from the Latin *nihil* – 'nothing', is a term for the philosophical idea that is a denial of existence or the denial of an objective basis for any truth.

We are human, made of human nature that inhabits a mortal body. Sometimes it is necessary to 'un-wind'. I know from my own experience, as you may also, that I have to have a less mentally stimulating activity prior to going to bed – otherwise the mind is still racing along at a pace that is not conducive to sleep!

But the real *deep thinking* we are talking about in reflection with God is not so much that which affects our frail nature directly – but that which is in His words to us. The Word came down to us, our prayers go up to Him. Therefore it is this reflecting that makes our relationship more secure, more informed and more real to us every day.

You've probably had the experience of walking by a lake or a pond on a calm day and you notice the reflections on the water. Then suddenly you see a goldfish swimming around, and your heart jumps a little because you are so close to it and the discovery reveals that the fish is reflecting the light too. That's reflecting *more deeply*! It's going below the obvious or superficial surface.

The Word that we have from God is more than ink on paper, it's quite unlike any other book. And is an abundant, ever-giving resource for reflection in prayer.

We can read books on all sorts of topics, fiction or non-fiction and for the most part what they say is one-dimensional be it profound or otherwise. If we read 'the cat sat on the mat' (OK, laugh at my reading level if you must!), then that's all there is to it. The cat doesn't have or need a reason; the mat is not a metaphor, type or lesson. The sentence is a mere coming together of two nouns.

Books such as those of John Milton, C.S. Lewis or J.R.R. Tolkien may have secondary meanings or parallels to other events woven through their stories – true or not, believable or not. But only the Bible is an inexhaustible, *multi*-dimensional work for all time.

In sincerely studying the Word of God we soon find ourselves *immersed* in its ways. No matter how deeply we reflect we never reach the full depth. We can follow things forwards, backwards, along tangents and the Bible just keeps on giving and demanding more exploration.

So, likewise in prayer we can exercise the same reflection on what God really means to us. Expressing this is the goal – having thought about it in depth is the practice.

An everyday example would be prayer before a meal. We could say, "For what we are about to receive, may the LORD make us truly thankful. Amen." However, even in the most sincere hearts this is not really an expression of a depth of understanding and therefore true appreciation of what our Heavenly Father has blessed us with. There's nothing wrong with a prayer like this. But it hasn't much of the gracious imagination of someone who has thought in depth about the blessing.

He's an awesome God who has *literally* moved heaven and earth in their seasons, delivered the clouds and rains in their times, placed a fierce sun at just the right distance, created nutritious plants, animals and other edibles and made them all grow pretty much without any help from humans – just to sustain the miracle of creation that we are, for a few more small hours - until we need to replenish our feeble stores yet again.

This is reflecting more deeply, this is the kind of example we can apply to almost every type of expression when reflecting with God.

Reflect: To *bring something to be* such as credit or discredit

In our moments of reflection with God we can *bring credit to Him* for what He does which is a powerful thought.

No doubt you've heard the phrase, "He's a chip off the old block". In part it's often true. I can think of various ways in which my siblings and I have characteristics, approaches, ethics and of course genetic attributes that have been passed on. I sometimes catch myself gesturing or perhaps folding my arms as my father did. I notice my brother whistling while doing physical work like dad used to. Or hear my sister teaching her children mischievous ditties, the origin of which I should probably deny any knowledge of!

You are probably reflecting right now about how you see similar things in yourself or your family. Some may bring a smile to your face and others a frown. From your parents' side they see either a credit or discredit – whether they deserve it or not.

I think you get what I mean but I really want to drive this message home for you; so let's all pile in and go for a quick spin in the time-machine. If you don't mind, set the dial to AD33 while I fasten my seat-belt.

OK, we've arrived at the temple in Jerusalem. We'll pull over and park in a loading zone and jump out. Running up the steps we see there are already lots of people everywhere, some yelling to friends across the crowded temple court, others fussing animals around.

On one side, yes, over by the wall the crowd has gathered more densely, they seem to be quieter, trying to hear someone. We find a place and can soon see why they are here; they are listening to the words of the prophet from Galilee. Irritated temple officials are gathered on one side, fuming and frowning. They ask him if they should pay a tax to Caesar or not, whether there's a resurrection or not and generally try to give him a hard time.

Few people know it but this man is under terrible strain. He's not eaten for many hours, his feet are sore from walking a long way, his throat is dry from trying to speak to those at the back of the crowd who want to hear him and his brow is damp with sweat from sitting so long in the sun of late Spring.

Even fewer people know how emotionally fragile he is feeling, for they don't know the many hours he was up last night. And even if they knew about it, they couldn't possibly imagine the desperately deep anguish that he was trying to control – because his mind was from time to time thinking about a cruel, painful and pitiless death he knew was just a few days away.

We sit there for a long time watching. The scene is not the way we thought about it before. The faces of the disciples seem more distant than we imagined them; they seem tired if not almost bored. The people look less enthused than we imagined. The priests and authorities seem more sinister and menacing than we thought. And sitting here together you and I feel an awful amount of compassion for what this poor man is enduring.

After a long time the crowds begin to drift away. They're hungry and have heard as much as they think they want to know. Generally they all begin to go their own way, and soon there's only a few of us here.

The man from Galilee stands, obviously in a little discomfort for sitting so long. And then you do something I didn't expect!

The whole situation has affected you as much as I, and you get to your feet and approach him. As he straightens up you move closer and he notices that you want to tell him something. You shake your head slightly in great admiration, you can feel a tear welling in your eye, and you know your voice will probably be a little shaky but you're going to say what you want to anyway. And then you do… "Lord, you really are a chip off the old block!"

He looks slightly taken aback. I notice Andrew and Philip immediately deep in discussion about your accent. Peter's suddenly looking decidedly awake. As I look back, the man from Galilee holds out his hand to you. You take his hand and I start wondering how hard you may shake it. I needn't have worried. He takes your hand in his other hand, and your hand is embraced in his two. You look down; I realize I would have done the same, and see as you do that there are not yet the marks of the nails. You look up to him again.

He looks into your face with his warm, compassionate eyes and a steady, determined, most reassuring gaze. And I hear him say to you directly, "Thank you. That is the kindest thing anyone has said to me for a long time."

A few days later, a short time before he was arrested, the following words were part of *his* prayer to his Father:

> "Neither pray I for these alone, but **for them also which shall believe on me** through their word; That they *all* may be one; as thou, Father, art in me, and I in thee, that *they also* may be one in us: that the world may believe that thou hast sent me. And the glory which thou gavest me I have given *them*; that *they* may be one, even as we are one: I in *them*, and thou in me, that *they* may be made perfect in one; and that the world may know that thou hast sent me, and hast *loved them*, as thou hast loved me."

In reflection, I think he is indeed a credit to his Father.

And no, I don't really believe that the first thing you will say to your Lord when you do meet him face to face is that he's a chip off the old block. I just want to help you remember to act and reflect in your life and in your prayers that you too have a Heavenly Father. And we all have a wonderful opportunity in Christ Jesus to *credit* our Father in many ways – starting with a desire which we can express continually in prayer of that glorious calling to *be like Him*.

> "How great is the love the Father has lavished on us, that we should be called children of God! **And that is what we are!** The reason the world does not know us is that it did not know him. Dear friends, now we are children of God, and what we will be has not yet been made known. But we know that when he appears, **we shall be like him**, for we shall see him as he is."

And I reckon that's worth reflecting on!

So here are at least five aspects or characteristics we can all use to enrich our reflecting with God.

When in prayer we share reflection with God as a partnership of ideas. It's not just one-way traffic. It's not just how we think or feel, nor how God does. It's not about just what we want or God wants out of the exercise as if prayer were some kind of 'negotiation' – instead it's a partnership in communication.

In reflection with God we really are able to bring all these aspects of reflection together, we bring ourselves and God together in the 'act' of prayer. When we share our words and our thoughts with God we expect we will also be affected by this process.

Now remember the several aspects to prayer – praise, reflection and petition. We are just dealing with reflection at this time. When you go to God in prayer and hopefully over our discussion so far we are learning that we can do this as often as we like; we are sharing something very special with our Heavenly Father.

Investing your feelings

Take your feelings to God in prayer. His feelings are deeply felt in His word. We know them and we become acquainted with them as we read more of His word. It is an exciting volume – it stirs us up spiritually and gets us thinking about the things that we are so wonderfully blessed with.

When you pray, remember that God can understand your feelings. If you are down, depressed, troubled, ill, happy, excited, ecstatic, humbled – make all your feelings known in your prayer.

Someone may ask, "Why take feelings to God in prayer, surely He knows how a person feels?" True. However, to *apply* this logic would mean that no prayer was ever required, and surely that's not the case. Should we not confess our sins and ask for forgiveness? Should we not praise and thank God for our blessings, great or small just because He knows already we are happy with them?

Prayer is not a type of creed. It does not require a set pattern or fixed format. It's not something that must be uttered only in a chant with or without meaningless repetition. True prayer is never like that. Bring *yourself* into your prayer.

God has nowhere said, 'Pray to me and check your feelings at the door.' Actually He's said quite the opposite on many occasions. One example is that *'The Lord is close to the broken-hearted and saves those who are crushed in spirit.'* If He wants to be 'close' to *us* when we are feeling like this - why would we think He doesn't want us to be close to *Him*?!

He wants *all* of us, especially the vulnerable and intimate parts of our minds to be close to Him, to trust Him and to be one with Him.

I'm reminded of the story of a boss who had two employees act up on the same day. One turned up ten minutes late with a lame excuse and the boss really tore into him about his tardiness. Later in the day, the other employee messed up something he was working on, threw the most spectacular tantrum and hurled a nearby object making a rather noticeable hole in the wall. The boss looked up for a moment, raised one eye-brow as if to say, 'Is that really necessary?' - and then simply continued on with his work.

When someone asked him later about what seemed to them a disproportionate judgment between the two incidents, he replied, "One *works* here - the other one has a *life* here."

As you can see, the boss knew he could get something good out of the employee who was passionate about what he did, who cared about results and who brought not just himself but *his feelings* for what he was doing to the job. The boss knew that the diamond was rough and he was supremely confident that all the guidance required was a simple raising of an eye-brow. The employee's own steam would get him the rest of the way.

God created our feelings, He knows them well. His great work is in actively bringing His creation back into the unity that existed in Eden - back to full reconciliation and full relationship with Him.

If you are worried about something, take it to God in prayer. Don't just take the facts to God in prayer, but also our feelings because when we do that we are reflecting the *reality* of our situation with God.

God can understand us; yes, He is a great being that dwells in light unapproachable but only the light is unapproachable – not God, by this gift of prayer. We can be with God in prayer and put ourselves into what we *give* God in prayer.

God can understand what each and every one of us is feeling. He knows how we feel. When we hold back our feelings in prayer and just present the simple facts, that is all it is – a bland presentation. We could almost do that as a third party. But this is not the case with true prayer. There are two parties involved – us and God. We need to remember to use feeling when we pray and be fully invested in our communication.

We choose what we will say to God but He knows what we will say before we even begin. Consider these words from 2 Chronicles 16:

> "For the eyes of the LORD run to and fro throughout the whole earth, to give strong support to those whose heart is perfect toward him."

How can our heart be perfect toward Him if we do not share the feelings of our heart? We will never be physically, emotionally or spiritually perfect before God (especially spiritually!). It's impossible for us as human beings – sinful, dying, troubled yet 'hopeful' human beings - to be perfect. But to be perfect in heart is to be *open* to God.

Talking with a God who knows everything

In Isaiah we read these words;

> "And it shall come to pass, that before they call, I will answer; and while they are yet speaking, I will hear."

And again in The Psalms;

"Before a word is on my tongue - you, Lord, know it completely."

So it begs the question once again; why pray to God if He already knows what we are going to say? Why pray to God if He in His foreknowledge knows all the words which we will form? What's the point of articulating?

Let's ask some other questions that may give another aspect: If God knows we have sinned (which He always does!) before we even ask forgiveness - should we ask for forgiveness or not? Our Heavenly Father knows our aspirations before we decide to disclose them to Him - should we ask Him to encourage us?

There will always be occasions in our lives when the most obvious thing we can do is pray. Last Wednesday I went to the supermarket and among other things bought a roast turkey roll; God knew that. Later that night I ate the roast turkey roll, as I had several times before – but apparently without reheating it properly; God knew that. In fact, I asked a blessing on the meal; God heard that too.

Thursday morning I awoke to a very severe case of food poisoning; God knew that. I'll spare you the unpleasant details as to how the body reacts to rampant bio-toxins waging war with a bunch of equally determined human immunoglobulin - and it's not what first comes to mind when I think of the term 'fun'; God knew that too.

Fourteen disagreeable hours later the battle was over and I fell into a long, rather well earned sleep; God knew that too. The following day I was still feeling rather fragile as I went about what seemed an enormous effort of disinfecting dishes, kitchen, bathroom, washing sweat-soaked bedding and generally returning the home to a state of liveable tranquillity. A nice hot shower was also a pleasant experience after the marathon ordeal.

That following morning, going about what I usually do, I reflected on how well I slept last night and I thanked God for a good night's rest. It really was a good sleep, and my frail body was probably still a little in need of it after recent events. But it really struck me as I said those words, and I said them out loud, that just hearing the words of that prayer seemed to fill the room with their sound.

It was obviously the recent event that had made me contrast in my mind those prayers throughout a painful trial (in which I thought more than once I was closer to death than I remember being in a long time!) with those prayers said in the relative quietude of a normal morning. Articulating thanksgiving for a night of rest actually seemed as present and confident as a prayer cried out in pain.

In a state of acute mortality, when the simple act of breathing was difficult, even praying aloud was painful. But I had no doubt my prayer was being heard. And so it struck me that having recovered and offering thanksgiving for something as mundane as sleep was no less heard than any other prayer – but *saying it made me aware* of it.

Moses spoke in the very near presence of God, as did Jonah in the bowels of an oceanic behemoth at the bottom of the sea – both were heard loud and clear. Jesus prayed on the top of a cold mountain, Daniel did in a den packed with lions – both were heard loud and clear. God knows the thoughts and intents of the heart; He knows what we are thinking. Yet all these faithful people prayed *even though* they were acutely aware that God knew where they were and what they were thinking.

Taking our thoughts, exposing them, and articulating them is *joining our thoughts with His knowledge*. And that's a very powerful part of a very divinely inspired relationship.

When we articulate our thoughts to God as well as our feelings, we are empowered with them. And so we should always take such thoughts to God in prayer.

There should be no exceptions to this. There are very few reasons why we shouldn't pray; sure there may be barriers occasionally, which are usually of our own making like those of sin and guilt – but these are barriers made for overcoming.

When we read the Bible, it's actually difficult to find occasions when people shouldn't have prayed. That's just how open the prayer channel is to us each and every moment of our lives. We should take more opportunities to pray and use prayer to join our thoughts and life's experience together with God's knowledge.

God hears the prayers of children

You know well the words of Christ in the Gospel of Matthew Chapter 18,

> "See that you do not despise one of these little ones. For I tell you that in heaven their angels always see the face of my Father who is in heaven."

We need to make two points about this aspect of reflection with God: Firstly, encourage children to pray more. The second is that in our prayers we should be more like a child. That's not really so hard to do – when we pray we are talking with our Heavenly 'Father.'

Being more like a child in prayer means taking the place of a child – not the father, mother, student, worker, boss, manager, professional, amateur, whatever else we see ourselves as – but as God does; 'we are the offspring of God.'

There's a way to approach this though. We are not to be childish but child-like. The former represents immaturity; the latter, the maturity to learn and desire to grow up spiritually. The former attitude prays 'Why me?' The latter prays, 'What else do I need to learn?'

Just as children reflect on what happens in and around their world, we should be able to approach God in the same way and it's worth all the encouragement in the world to do so because God hears a child's prayer, young or old.

Perhaps as a child you remember or have heard of the 'Children's bedtime prayer':

> Bless me LORD this night I pray
> Keep me safe till dawn of day
> Bless my mother and my father
> Bless my sister and my brother
> Bless each little girl and boy
> Bless them all for heavenly joy.

It's a simple prayer that when we break down the simple aspects of it line by line surely demonstrates to us a good example of reflection in prayer.

I encourage you to listen to a child's prayer very carefully. Let me give you an example. My sister and her husband and their two-year-old were recently staying with me. My little niece happened to be quite taken with the words of the song 'You raise me up.' I forget the words, but my little niece knew a couple of lines. With her little two year old voice she liked to belt out the one line she really had a handle on, "You raise meee UUUP!"

Her uncle was greatly amused. A couple of months later the family came back for yet another visit which is always delightful. My sister shared a story with me. Each meal that her children sit down to, they are encouraged to offer thanksgiving for the food they are about to eat. It's a simple prayer for the little children, 'Dear God, thank you for my breakfast/lunch/dinner, Amen'. They're still quite young so a short prayer is a big achievement.

Then one day, while driving with her mother my niece, from the back of the vehicle decided that it was as good a time as any to exercise her ability to reflect with God. And so was heard the little voice in the back seat, "Dear God, You raise meee-UUUP! Amen."

Can you reflect with God like that? As simple as the little prayer was it has the elements of reflecting with God. This dear little child took all the things that she knew to be relevant between her and God and expressed them. In three little sentences admittedly – but we can do that and more.

We know that God hears the prayers of children. Of course we know that there are some things that they cannot ask for until they come to Christ; yet God hears a child's prayer and it is good to encourage them to pray.

It's wise to always listen to a child's prayer carefully and become good at praying with our own child-like faith to our Heavenly Father.

Reflection must always leave us dependent

When we were looking at praise with God we laid down a foundation that gave us guidance for praise with God. In reflections with God we also need a foundation on which we can build our understanding. That is simply this: Reflection with God must always leave us *dependent* on God.

When we reflect with God we express and put before Him the fact that we can't do it all by ourselves, we are getting better at what we are doing and we are hopeful of being more spiritual in the way we go about it. However, we will never be able to do everything entirely by ourselves.

It defeats the purpose of prayer to think, 'I can do everything, it's all in my control - but I am going to pray to God for help.' As soon as we admit that we need God or as soon as we give God the glory or honour we are no longer independent. Prayer and particularly reflection in prayer will always leave us dependent on God.

It might be a small prayer for a small matter or it might be a large prayer for a larger matter. A prayer may be a long prayer about one single subject or issue or a short prayer about one tiny problem; yet in that prayer we must always acknowledge that we will be dependent on God.

This, as in praise, is a foundation for reflection with God. And so we can see, as dependent as we will always be on God, there is therefore really very little that we cannot take to God in prayer.

Take the example of someone who is 'feeling low' (spiritually or emotionally, perhaps physically) – we can always take a broken heart to God for repair. Sometimes we are more apt to pray when we are at a loss – and that of course is not the only time when we should pray. But no matter what happens, whatever state we find ourselves in we can always be ready to take a broken heart to God in prayer. The Psalmist says this actually;

> "The LORD is near to the brokenhearted and saves the contrite in spirit."

It's almost a prerequisite to prayer, not that we always have a broken heart but that we are of a contrite spirit. It takes a lot of reflection to be 'contrite.' Always having an element of contrition in our reflection acts as a safety switch to our *respect* in prayer. We don't have to feel low about it or down about it – humility is itself a wonderful tool for working upon the human spirit and for opening our hearts, expressing our words and taking our feelings in truth to God in prayer.

What I like about this phrase from the Psalms is that it so eloquently expresses the situations that we really do find in life. Brokenhearted is the state in which circumstances have 'happened' to us - someone or something made us feel this way.

Instead, being *contrite* is a state that we have control of; before or after we need to. Unlike being brokenhearted it's something we have a choice about. Isn't it satisfying to be able to *do* something active or pro-active?

Tell God your fears

One thing that I have found interesting in my own reflection with God is that He has no fear. It may sound obvious but have you ever stopped and really thought about this? All the fears and worries that we have in our lives, He just doesn't have. Certainly, He can understand them - but God doesn't have any fear. We can take our fears to God and He will understand them.

Isn't this an interesting opportunity? Isn't this an exciting thing to be able to do? As a child you may have been afraid of the dark and you could always call on your parents who would come to you and turn the light on. Yet we get a *little* bit older, a *little* bit wiser in the way of the world – and a *lot* more worried. We've found a lot more fears which we keep and harbour, and we forget what it was once like to approach our Father with our fears.

Tell God your fears, He can understand them and talking through your fears with Him is a very real, very productive and very sure way of dealing with them. Never be 'afraid' to take your fears to God. It's a healing process for all of us. There are some things I'd never share with people who are even the closest to me because I'd worry about my fear creating in them a feeling of fear (for me or them). With God none of us has to worry about this.

Sometimes we are afraid of very small things: Spiders, sharks, fear of the dark, a fear of heights. Wherever we are and whatever we fear we can take all of them to God. And you know what? God *wants* to hear about them all. He really does, because you can't be who you are to Him and reflect with Him until you do!

I was once told the story of a preacher by the name of Morgan. I've remembered this story because it really gave me perspective for how kind God is; and the attention to detail of which He is capable. A woman once asked Morgan, "Sir, do think we ought to pray even about the little things in life?" Mr. Morgan in an understated yet reassuring manner replied, "Madam, can you think of anything in your life that is *big* to God?"

What about us, can we think of anything in our life that is big to God?

If we were to take world famine to God, He would not be overwhelmed by the challenge. If we were to take world poverty to God, He would not be overawed by the challenge. If we were to take world peace to God – would He not be able to hear it? And we think these are the *big* things.

There is nothing in our life that is too big for God. So, don't sweat on the small stuff – just take it to God. And together with Him, reflect on it and understand that there is nothing in our life too large or too small for God to hear in prayer.

Talk about your weaknesses

We all have them. Reflect on them with God. Tell God, 'I really want to do this but I feel I am not able. I know you have strength that I do not have and your strength is made perfect in my weakness. Where I am weak, you are strong.' Reflect on this regularly with your Heavenly Father.

Of course, we all have times in our lives when we fall short of our calling, we fall short of our Heavenly Father's expectations, and we fall short of our own standards and expectations. We sin and slip-up and these are very important moments on which to reflect with God.

Forgiveness is a great blessing but one that is useless to us if we don't seek it in prayer. Although it is unhealthy to dwell on negative behaviour, immoral or un-spiritual matters past or present too much, we should go to God openly and say, 'God, I did this, and I am responsible for it. I'm reflecting with you at this time so that I will have the strength not to do it again and I will learn to behave and think like you and your ways. I will reflect more of you and your virtues instead of sitting here holding my values and ignoring what is right in you.'

Have you ever spent time thinking about the difference between a value and a virtue? A value is something that 'we believe' but a virtue is something that 'we do.' You've heard the old saying,

> Patience is a virtue, possess it if you can,
> seldom found in women and never found in man.

Patience is an action. It's something we actually do, even though we often don't think we are doing something, we are; we are being patient. That's a virtue.

Values are things that we believe but virtues are things that we *do*. We need to take our values to God in prayer that we may be strengthened to act on them as virtues in our lives. Do that and see God lift the burden of weakness!

Consider Psalm 38, an important part of the Word. It's not the most positive or pretty picture from Scripture - but it is real and a very good example of sin, forgiveness and reflecting with God;

> "There is no soundness in my flesh because of your indignation; there is no health in my bones because of my sin. For my iniquities have gone over my head; like a heavy burden, they are too heavy for me. My wounds stink and fester because of my foolishness."

He doesn't say 'because of my bad luck' but because of 'my own foolishness.' See how the Psalmist is reflecting in this way. He's not just saying, 'I've sinned and therefore you are expecting me to ask for forgiveness'; he's examining the cause and he's reflecting with God as to why it happened. And in endeavouring to change this, he is reflecting together with God. He continues,

> "I am utterly bowed down and prostrate; all the day I go about mourning. For my sides are filled with burning, and there is no soundness in my flesh. I am feeble and crushed; I roared because of the tumult of my heart."

'I roared,' he says 'because of the disquietness of my heart.' Can I ask you a personal question; have you ever prayed to God at 'full volume'? Have you ever prayed to God at the top of your voice? I have, at least a couple of times. The writer is not finished; listen to these words in Psalm 38,

> "O Lord, all my longing is before you; my sighing is not hidden from you. My heart throbs; my strength fails me, and the light of my eyes - it also has gone from me."

Consider the absolute depths of the feelings that the Psalmist is sharing in reflection with God. Can we do this? Have we done it? Can we do it again? I encourage you to embrace this kind of depth of reflection with God. It's raw, intense, personally affected.

> "My friends and companions stand aloof from my plague, and my nearest kin stand far off. Those who seek my life lay their snares; those who seek my hurt speak of ruin and meditate treachery all day long."

Have you ever thought that someone thinks you're not all you're made out to be? Or does not have a good opinion of you? Are you worried they've got it in for you? Maybe it's a co-worker, or an associate, a friend or someone at school or college, even a loved one - and you are worried about their demeanour towards you.

Look at what the Psalmist does about this. He takes it to God and reflects on what is happening in his life. And his problems were probably a lot bigger than ours.

> "But I am like a deaf man; I do not hear, like a mute man who does not open his mouth. I have become like a man who does not hear, and in whose mouth are no rebukes. But for you, O LORD, do I wait; it is you, O Lord my God, who will answer. For I said, "Only let them not rejoice over me, who boast against me when my foot slips!" For I am ready to fall, and my pain is ever before me. I confess my iniquity; I am sorry for my sin."

It sounds depressing - but so is sin. So is iniquity and transgression because they are out of step with strong spiritual virtue. But we can and should share this with God. In fact, Psalm 55 says,

> "Cast your burden on the LORD, and he will sustain you; he will never permit the righteous to be moved."

We are encouraged because God can take what we are saying to Him and remove it from the relationship that we share. Isn't that what we desire when we confess our sins and weaknesses to Him? And let that, like the Psalmist said, be all our desire.

To be close to you dear Heavenly Father – and to be closer without this horrible burden of sin, and to know that we can be as close to you as we like; and yet each and every time we off-load our burden to you, each time you cast it from us, you will catch it and remove it as far as east is from west. And remember it no more, and that is your great strength to us.

Talk about your strengths with God

Just as our weaknesses can undo us; so too can our strengths if we trust in them alone or place the wrong emphasis on them. So we need to talk about our strengths, talk about what we have, count them out loud as blessings and ask God to preserve them for good. In all of us there is a tendency, when we are alone, even in a busy place, to think that we have an advantage that is ours alone. And that is just the time to talk to God about our strengths. Ask that they may always be used for good and thank God for them.

Reflecting with God requires us to express our feelings with God and our relationship with him. It's difficult to do that if we don't believe He is there for us in our lives. Psalm 4 says,

> "Stand in awe, and sin not: commune with your own heart upon your bed, and be still. Selah."

That is something to reflect upon. In fact, the Psalmist follows these words with the word 'Selah' - and a rough English translation of the Hebrew word means, 'Stop and think'. Or in our case for the purpose of our considerations here – 'stop and reflect'. In our day we should stop and reflect with God as to the source of all strength. Selah.

Open your Bible

Pray often with your Bible open. It contains God's words which He speaks to you, me and anyone else who can open a Bible, which is pretty much all humanity. And He speaks to us through this medium as often as we simply open and read it. Practise praying with your Bible open because we are really opening the line a little more so it's not all about what we have to say to God and what we think He wants to hear. Open, read, hear and pray.

Consider this old saying,

> Little of the Word with little prayer is death to spiritual life.
> Much of the Word with little prayer gives a sickly life.
> Much prayer with little of the Word gives an emotional life.
> But a full measure of both the Word and prayer each day gives a healthy and powerful life. [2]

They are deep words; simple but profound. It's almost a tongue twister. See if you can say this quickly! It's worth learning this little saying to remember the wisdom for later.

An easy way to pray and read at the same time is to just simply read the prayers that are in the Bible. If you haven't yet had time to count how many there are to choose from – there's around 650! The Psalms of course are rich in this area. As you read put yourself in that prayer, and pray 'through' it to God.

The essence of the message is pray AND read.

---

[2] Attributed to Andrew Murray, a South African reformist preacher of the mid 1800's.

Prayer Heroes

Find in God's word 'Prayer Heroes'. These are men and women, faithful of old, who have prayed to God. So, find your own prayer hero. Perhaps you'll need different ones at different times.

To be honest, I have a couple because I think they are all great examples. Sometimes one gives me more encouragement than at other times. Sometimes one has the direction I need but we all have plenty to choose from in Scripture, men and women alike. Some of the most inspirational incidents are where prayer heroes like Hannah, Deborah and Mary talked with God. There are really big prayers by Hezekiah, David, Solomon –plenty of great examples for us to select from and use to build-up our own prayer experience.

There are of course the prayers of our Lord Jesus Christ who prayed over some small things compared to what he was in his life, and certainly compared to what he endured. We can take examples, both from the Old and New Testaments and expand on them. So find yourself a couple of prayer heroes in the Word.

It's not just the characters of these people of prayer that are important for us to note but that they were human just like us. They faced problems we also face. Some are dramatic, like praying for a dying child. I know people in my life who have done that – imagine what it felt like for a parent three or four thousand years ago – without modern medicine to 'assist' God's intervention. How many more examples of things prayed for greater or smaller than this do we find in Scripture?

A new lesson from an old gardener

I'd like to share another story with you, perhaps you'll be interested in doing this too. There was an old sister who was unable to look after her property anymore and she had a very big garden at the back of her house. Being elderly she was no longer able to mow lawns, cut hedges, dig holes and plant flower beds. Consequently a lot of the garden became over-run. But once while visiting her and walking through the garden with her we came across a small patch of garden that was immaculately cared for.

It wasn't very big at all but it was tidy and pretty. It was swept and clean. There was nothing growing there that was unwanted, such as weeds. Compared to the rest of the garden though it was tiny, almost insignificant really.

I asked the sister why this little part of the garden was important to her. I expected her to say something along the lines of that's where my husband was sitting when he died or I have a special memory in this part of the garden. Instead she simply answered, "This is my *prayer garden*."

And that was where she went to reflect with God. Everything else in her garden was too big, too hard and too far - she couldn't physically care for it any more. But there was one small patch of her life where she was able to share with God. There was one place she always had the strength to keep tidy and spiritually fruitful.

You may like to make yourself a prayer garden. You could say, 'Oh forget about it, I don't have a garden,' or 'I live in an apartment' – that's fine, get yourself a couple of pots and stick something green, alive and *dependent* in them.

Perhaps you rent and are not responsible for a garden. That's fine too but just take a small patch and go there regularly and reflect with God. It doesn't have to be grand because it will still not be big enough to God - it just has to fit you in it *for* Him.

But it will be special, it will be yours and you will be able to reflect with God in that place. Because when you are there you will be reminded that everything in that place is dependent on God, that everything there God cares for, and everything is growing – including you. It's growing because it's reflecting the *peace*, the *hope*, and the *strength* of a Heavenly Father who does care.

And if by a small measure and if in a simple way we are to achieve something great, it will be to reflect those three things; peace, hope and strength - and grow!

~ 4 ~
PETITION *with* GOD

Ears that hear

In this section we will look at petition with God together. The key verse for our considerations is from Psalm 143;

> "Hear my prayer, O LORD, give ear to my supplications."

What is interesting about this verse is that it positions us automatically in God's will. It meets the criteria of many aspects that we have already considered as the foundation stones to prayer. One of those is that prayer will always leave us dependent on God. Of course, if God were to 'give ear' it is because we are dependent on Him hearing us - we *are* His dependants.

Later we will look at answers with God; here want to be specific in looking at only petition with God. The two are not easily separated. Those words 'give ear to my supplications' reminds us that God hears prayer. It's still up to God as to what He does about it from there. Nevertheless we are always heard by God.

We may ask, 'Well, what's the use of Him hearing us but not giving us what we want?' I think when we reflect on all the blessings in our lives there are many times when He does indeed give us what we want and many times what we ask for. In reality though, He actually gives us far more than what we think or even know to ask for.

Belief and petition

Sometimes we hold ourselves back because we think our belief is not strong enough or our faith is not strong enough to believe that we can ask God for something – even small things. There is nothing in our lives 'too big' for God and there is nothing 'too small' to take to Him in prayer.

We need to differentiate between the difference of having the courage to believe - and the disregard for God's will in favour of our own expectations. The story is well told, unfortunately it is too common, of the fundamentalist pastors who tell parents of sick children to pray and everything will be all right – and when it is not and the child dies, they blame the parents and tell them they didn't pray hard enough, often enough or believe enough. Shameful ignorance!

There is nothing we cannot ask God for in fact, He asks us to ask. But there is nothing God is committed to give outside of His will. It's that simple.

> **Petition**: Noun. A request made for something desired, especially a respectful or humble request, as to a superior or to one in authority; a supplication or prayer; a petition for aid; a petition to God for courage and strength.

No matter what value petitioners place on the petition, it remains in the purview of the petitioned as to whether to give it or not. If you ask me for a dollar and I refuse and you get angry at me; you are not petitioning - you are demanding. Demands are not always going to be parallel with God's will or ideals.

But this is really good news when we think about it. We have a God who actually knows what He is doing! That is an even more sure reason to have faith when we pray. It gives us greater confidence that God is able to perform His will and that we can and do *fit* inside that plan. Therefore we have greater confidence that He is a God we can believe in.

My ways

Belief that we have a God who can hear, who can be petitioned, who we can trust to answer us in the best possible way means that we are no longer small or narrow focused individuals – instead we are teachable and open-minded to enormous spiritual potential.

Here's an example. I'm going to pray that God will give me someone to preach to today. That sounds pretty much like one of the best things we could petition God for; right? So I step out the front door just as a vehicle doing a little over the limit swerves to miss a cat and clips me as it bounds over the verge.

'Imagine that,' says God, 'I knew the little fellow was serious when he asked me to let him preach. So I've given him four weeks off work so he can preach to the guy in the hospital bed next to him!'

We didn't see that coming. We were sincere – but are we open to the real answer? As God tells Isaiah:

> "My thoughts are not your thoughts, and your ways are not My ways."

This is not to say that we should take the example too seriously. We shouldn't avoid petitioning for opportunities to speak to others of Him for fear of being hit by a bus. The example is just one to get us thinking again that God has no fear and can deliver us from any situation – even from death itself. And that the fearless God we petition has an eminently wonderful mind with thoughts and ways we can only admire. Meditating in such a way will make us stronger, more open, more prayerful and consistent in *our ways*.

God's ways are consistent with His will. He knows all about our will – some of it will be similar to His, some of it will not be. The big picture is that His will is far grander than we could possibly imagine. Faith diminishes in proportion to the distance we are removed from God's will. His way is to always stir things up a little so we can see that proportion. True faith expects to be challenged – and not fear change.

Life to us is largely watching things whiz by as we gaze out the side window of the vehicle. Life to God is more looking out the front windscreen, a long way down the road, He always knows what is coming up long before it whips past the side window confusing the proportion and making us think things are moving faster than what is indicated on the speedometer.

But we're spiritual kids, we can't see over the front seat and so the driver wants us to trust Him because He *can* see. We don't know the twists or the turns, we don't know the day nor the hour, we don't know the distance run or the time of arrival – what we do know is that whatever happens we're going to arrive in the same place because we are *with* God.

Do you have a relationship?

It is wonderful to *share* our lives with our Heavenly Father. Sharing is an intrinsically vital element of our relationship with Him. The relationships we have in this mortal system, husbands and wives, parents and children, friends and fellows are a glimpse of what we have with God – which is why we have them.

Of course, we have many other relationships in this world that are far less important than the one we have with our Heavenly Father. I have a relationship with the electricity company. Every month or so they send me a letter reminding me that they're still thinking about me, and that they would like me to contribute to their bank account. Quite unexpectedly these thoughtful letters arrive and I put them on a little pile, usually until they send me another letter and then I write back to them, thank them for their thoughtfulness and enclose a cheque.

Our relationship with God isn't like that. He doesn't need to know that we still love Him for He knows that whether we express it or not. He doesn't need us to write letters to Him either – but He wants us to ask. He wants us to open our hearts to Him – open our minds and make our best contribution in communicating with Him, as a Father.

Quite unlike the letters that arrive from the electricity company our prayers don't just turn-up unannounced to God. They don't just *arrive* out of the blue. Our most faithful friend and great example, the Lord Jesus Christ – when we ask in his name – can personally deliver each and every prayer, each praise, each reflection and each petition to our Heavenly Father.

In Hebrews chapter 9 we read:

> "For Christ is not entered into the holy places made with hands, which are the figures of the true; but into heaven itself, now to appear in the presence of God for us."

We have a faithful Father in God, a faithful Mediator in Christ – they need us to close the circle and make the relationship complete.

Family

So what can we take to God in petition? We can take everything to God in prayer. Let's look at a few simple examples of things that we can do in our prayer lives – prayer-full lives – to grow and to understand all the things that we can ask for and can share with our Heavenly Father.

Firstly, pray for *all* your family and friends. We need to do this on a very regular basis because sharing our relationship with each other, our family and friends whether they be son, daughter, wife, husband, girlfriend, boyfriend, child, aunt, uncle, grandparent – whoever we are close to, pray about these people regularly because their lives affect our lives more than most other people we encounter.

When we pray for a brother or a sister, a mother or a father we are taking to God the aspects of our relationships that affect us most. When we are sharing that with God and asking Him, or petitioning Him to bless the person who is close to us and those with whom we share our lives on a regular basis – then we are reinforcing *relationship principles* in prayer. So it's very important to pray for our family, if not first in our prayers, then soon thereafter.

Relationships, particularly those of family, are a shadow or a type of the relationship we have with God. Therefore they teach us responsibility, care, love, compassion, wisdom and many other relationship principles that can be translated from our natural lives to our spiritual ones.

So this practice often sets a tone for how we petition God. Also, it helps us to pray for needs that we know of and people who have that need.

Friends

We have by design a situation that when we are praying for people that are in our lives we are automatically asking God to be involved in the things that we are doing and the people we are sharing that *doing* with. Always pray for your friends - be they those who are in the assembly, or people you are dealing with daily anywhere else.

These two groups of people, family and friends, are those that most open our heart and most concentrate our mind on what we are taking to God.

If you are like me you probably know a lot of people, which is quite a phenomenon in our life in the Lord – we actually meet many people.

I read a news article recently in which a scientist reckoned that humans can only recognise (remember) around an hundred and fifty names and faces. The scientists sure didn't ask me! I think that number is dead-wrong.

There are teachers who know every child in the school. There are sales representatives who know the names and faces of everyone of hundreds of customers, as well as their employees. Sports-casters call every name of every player in the league as well as their stats. I can think of a dozen other examples of everyday people who can recognize more than an hundred and fifty names and faces – nurses are another, they routinely remember everyone in the hospital, staff and patients alike!

I know the names and faces of thousands of brothers and sisters around the world – and there's nothing unique about me! In considering prayer it's worth remembering that God knows all of them – past and present. Making His care *our* care in prayer is an important part of growing our relationship with God as well as our brothers and sisters in faith.

We have a lot of people to pray for and to care about whether they share our faith or share our lives in another way.

Daily prayer for daily people

Another idea for something that we can actually do about our prayer life is to get a calendar and write-in all the birthdays of all the people that you know. It's a good exercise to find out the birthdays of the people you know. Write them on the calendar and pray for that person especially on that day.

Now, here's the interesting part; in between all the days with a birthday on them write in those days the name of someone else you know and every day you will have someone to pray for.

We may have many people we pray for often in our day such as family and friends, so get a calendar, put it on the wall, somewhere you will walk by often and write in the names of those people you know – you will be surprised how many people you know. Even just one person for each day will prove the scientist wrong again. You will also be surprised how this practice will enliven, invigorate and refresh your life in prayer.

When you see all those names as you add them (and pray for them!) a remarkable thing will happen. You will experience the recognition of being surrounded by people you know, love and care for – and the blessing is quite amazing when you see it presented like this!

Enemies and burdens

It's difficult to pray for our enemies – those who hurt us or stand against us. We can look at some of the Psalms to read of the difficulty David had in expressing prayer for his enemies. Yet Jesus Christ encourages us to pray for those who don't do well by us.

When we do pray and have sincerely asked God to bless a person who may not need (or even like!) our asking for a blessing for them, it builds a character that strengthens our spiritual minds. This practice also relieves us of the burdens of guilt, hate, envy, jealousy and of all these enervating thoughts that sour our minds. We all know these feelings.

When we petition God for our enemies we 'turn that out' of ourselves so we are once again free to move on. Praying for our enemies is the second best way to do to relieve our emotional burdens after asking for forgiveness for ourselves. Having asked for forgiveness we are free from the burden of sin. Christ encourages us to be free from any emotional burdens that we also carry in relation to our enemies.

This is something to keep up regularly and unburden ourselves of these feelings and cast off or shed those feelings of guilt and shame at every opportunity in prayer.

Of course, if you don't have any enemies I'm not going to recommend you make some just to enjoy a more fulfilling prayer life! ...so, just pray for some of mine instead.

Praying for the unknown

Another petition that we can bring before God is to pray for someone you have never met. We may hear of someone who is close to somebody else or is related to somebody and we can pray for them. This is particularly easy to do because there are many things that we may be involved in at a distance such as mission or outreach work.

This kind of prayer won't surprise God but the blessing may just turn-up for the person we are praying for. And you know the sweetest thing about that? We may never know that it was answered! We may never know whether God answered that prayer but we'll do it again and again. Because it is a part of our being, our spiritual life, to desire the best for those who may not share prayer with God as we do – so let's pray for someone we've never met.

Let go of the need for self

Pray to God in many of your prayers asking nothing for yourself. Think carefully about that - and ask yourself this question, 'When was the last time I prayed to God, or petitioned God, and didn't ask something for myself?' Some of you reading this are probably shaking your heads; I guarantee there are more of us who can't remember the last time we prayed to God asking nothing for ourselves than those of us who can.

Jesus Christ often prayed asking nothing for himself, as did the Apostle Paul on many occasions. Practise praying to God and sharing petition with God but not selfishly. It probably goes without saying that selfishness and prayer don't really fit in well with the will of God. We do depend on God and we should thank Him. We do need His help and we can ask Him for anything we like - but selfishness is mutually exclusive to a spiritual life and mutually exclusive to positioning ourselves in God's will.

I'm not saying that we should never pray asking God for something for ourselves, which is an extreme I am not advocating. But petitioning God *often*, and asking nothing for ourselves helps us to grow spiritually. It also prompts us to ask for the right things, for the right reasons when we *do* pray for those things that we need personally.

Talking with God often is what changes our attitude and perspective. If it's our habit to talk about everything with God we lose our doubt or fear that He isn't listening. When we hit one big bump in the road we don't compress all our untried expectations into one lump of negativity – instead we are accustomed to keeping on and we don't get *change paralysis*. We let go of what our doubt controls and rest instead on God's supreme control of all situations.

When flying from A to B the pilot calls-in all the time, he doesn't panic and yell 'Mayday' *only* when something goes wrong. God is in control – call-in often.

Taking joint responsibility

Often pray for God to bless someone – then go and *do* something for that person yourself. In our relationship with God, when we acknowledge that we are dependent on Him – and true prayer always acknowledges that we are dependent on God – we can enlarge on this relationship with our Heavenly Father by *participation* in His will.

You see, if sister So-and-so needs help financially, I can petition God on her behalf. Meanwhile, if I go and secretly place $20 in an envelope and put it in her letter box when I know she's at work (or cannot see me do it!) how much has that prayer been answered already? You may say I could have put the money in the letter box and not prayed to God - but the little I can afford is not going to fix all her problems.

But doing this positions the petitioner (me in this case) *in* the will of God because I am participating in His will and His will *is* to bless that sister. Petition for God often to bless someone – then *go* and do something for them yourself.

Someone may say, 'Well, that's just playing games with God's will.' But let me ask you a question: '*Who* blessed me with that $20?' And, '*Who* gave *me* the free will to choose what I do with it?'

If one answers, 'God' to either of those two questions – it's not a game, it's a partnership and a relationship built on very firm spiritual foundations!

It doesn't have to be money. We can pray for someone and then pick-up the phone and ask them if they are feeling better. I wouldn't bother keeping a scorecard, but you'd be surprised how many people find out their prayer for someone else was immediately answered. Of course, sometimes it was answered before we even thought to pray – but finding out, well isn't that just as good a reminder that God has us in His thoughts also?

Sometimes help is unappreciated or misunderstood but blessings don't always go unnoticed and we should be mindful and spiritually ready to act on as many of our prayers as we can.

Petition God earnestly in prayer for something that we have no control over and that will not benefit us personally. Asking God earnestly for something we have no control over embraces those things that we have been considering and also leaves us dependent on God whether or not He fulfils these petitions –as we ask for them or just as He sees they are required. Contributing is *Working with God*.

Incense

One thing I like to visualise in my prayers and that I encourage others to try also is to imagine my prayers ascending gently to God like incense. It reminds us of the way incense was used as a type of prayer in Scripture. For those who have burnt or seen incense burnt, it gently *drifts* upward. Petition God and imagine your petition ascending like incense if it concerns *you* – and imagine it ascending like email if it concerns *someone else*. I find the practice develops trust and patience – both of which I'll take as much as I can get!

In other words, take upon yourself the humility and the faith that God will answer your prayers but have an urgency about prayer, a desire in your prayer that others are provided for also. This was very much how Christ prayed. Although he had an enormous requirement for spiritual strength himself - it was the spirit of Christ, not the Spirit to perform miracles, but the spiritual character of the man that others were always considered first.

These are things in prayer that take a bit of practice. We need to form new and healthy spiritual habits to take our prayer lives forward and to grow in our hope and in the love that we share together, and in the faith that our Heavenly Father will do as He will. This practice aligns us with this spiritual development. Exercise these things in prayer and gain a spiritual creativity.

Child's play

Improving our prayer life is a little bit like children learning to colour in. We give a child a colouring book and a pack of bright pencils, which is safer than giving them bright permanent markers because children don't always colour within the lines. Prayer is a bit like colouring in; we have this beautiful array of colours and we also have lines that we know are God's will. At other times it's not a line but a dot-dot-dot where we have to fill in a few gaps and perhaps guess where that line is and sometimes we learn that we honestly don't know. That's all right because we don't have to and are not expected to know all that God does.

But practising *helps* us to see the picture as a whole. And when we are humble or teachable as little children and we take to our prayer colouring book with our pens and pencils, we can be just like children with prayer. "God, can I ask you for anything? Can I draw anything I want? Can I colour this prayer green, and this one blue and this one black and this one - well I think it's a bit grey isn't it?" Prayer *is* colourful but just like a little child we need to fill it in and we need to use all the colours and this takes practice.

It takes practice to get from our first illustration on the refrigerator to the one hanging in the National Gallery. We all want our prayer lives hanging in the Gallery of God – but it takes practice and that means trying more creative disciplines. You know where that leads us - we have to pray more, we need to learn more about colours, textures, materials and emotions.

We have to learn we can't press too hard or our pencil goes through the canvas – we end up with a holey prayer life instead of the holy one we need. We have to practise prayer like a child with a canvass that is our life before the God with whom we are communicating– both *to* Him and *from* Him!

God has a wonderful imagination - some of the creatures in our world teach us that – prayer that reflects this imagination is a prayer that has dynamism and colour which is *lively*.

Honesty

Be honest in your prayers. We may ask, 'How could I not be honest in my prayers? God knows exactly what I'm thinking. It's no good me petitioning Him for a washing machine if He knows I need a cooker. It's no good me asking Him for help if I'm not serious about helping myself. God knows that.'

The human mind is capable of many little subtleties. Sometimes we need to stop during prayer and ask if we are being honest. It's not a matter of cheating God – that's never going to happen. But if we are not honest we can't position *ourselves* in God's will and therefore we can't grow within the prayer lives we desire.

And these things often take small and subtle forms that can mess with our own message or mind. For example I may say, 'God, I really need a better job - this one is killing me.' – and then I stop and say more honestly, 'Really God, I am blessed to have a job but I would *like* to do something else.'

There is a difference between 'I would *like* something else' and 'I *need* something else.' I'm not cheating God with the difference but I am subtly deluding myself as to my actual requirement – and therefore my expectation will be twisted as well. If I thought like this on a regular basis it wouldn't be long before it affected my perception and consequently my character.

Where the small matter of honesty in this example matters is that it's presumptuous of us to say we need a job when God has already blessed us with a means to earn our daily bread. We must instead assume that God already knows our needs and that we are dependent on Him for provision of all His blessings.

This honesty also leads us to ask whether God is much in our current circumstance. It allows us to ask in humility whether God has a purpose for us in this position.

This level of honesty in prayer soon permeates other areas of our lives. If we are right with God it's a safe bet we're going to be right with our relationships with others – not that they are going to be perfect but that we are going to be honest in our approach, reasonable in our expectations and wise in our actions.

Be specific - Be alive when you pray

Being specific reminds us of that foundation we discovered in the first chapter – prayer needs to be *articulated*. God knows far more of what we need than we will ever ask for but when we pray for things specifically we align ourselves in the relationship, in our faith and our expectations - and therefore God's will. Ultimately it's *us* God wants and therefore the specific things that make us or changes us to be the person God desires are the things we should remember to ask for.

And these are always specific things. There's no point in vaguely asking God to make us a better person. That will have no effect on us – therefore we are only vaguely placing ourselves in God's will. That won't do. Instead (I'll use myself as an example!) ask God to help tame a temper or give me confidence to speak. That's real. That kind of prayer has the potential to change a life or at least to begin to change a life – and that's exciting.

It is good to be animated in our prayers, to ask fervently, earnestly and with assurance - petition God in the same way that we would encourage even ourselves for something. The well known preacher Spurgeon once wrote;

> "Prayer pulls the rope down below and the great bell rings above in the ears of God. Some scarcely stir the bell, they pray so languidly. Others give only an occasional jerk of the rope. But he that communicates with heaven is the man who grasps the rope boldly and pulls continuously with all his might."

It's a great word picture. Just reading it again I'm going back over my prayers today. Honestly, I think a couple of them were lacking 'all my might' – note to self: improvement required.

Prayer that moves you

Develop prayer that has compassion and joy. It's OK to petition God in tears; you may have had this experience already. It reminds me of that shortest verse in the Bible, found in John 11:

> "Then when Mary was come where Jesus was, and saw him, she fell down at his feet, saying unto him, Lord, if thou hadst been here, my brother had not died. When Jesus therefore saw her weeping, and the Jews also weeping which came with her, he groaned in the spirit, and was troubled, And said, Where have ye laid him? They said unto him, Lord, come and see. Jesus wept."

This is a good example from the life of the Lord Jesus Christ; the Lord's need was not necessarily too heavy for *him* but it is OK to cry when we pray – in doing so there is compassion (or joy); his example is a clear moment of perspective.

Our Lord was not like a rock who went through his entire life unmoved by the emotions that he inherited in his flesh. He had the experience of laughter, joy, sadness and loss in his life. He knew exactly what these friends were going through; and he came to a point where he *wept*.

It's the shortest verse in the Bible that tells us that Jesus, in a moment when prayer was required, wept. But the story goes on,

> "Then said the Jews, Behold how he loved him!... Jesus therefore again groaning in himself cometh to the grave. It was a cave, and a stone lay upon it... Then they took away the stone from the place where the dead was laid. And Jesus lifted up his eyes, and said, Father, I thank thee that thou hast heard me."

John in his Gospel stresses that *again* Jesus has been *more* affected, *again* emotionally invested in the moment because he had that same compassion we all have by our nature. When they remove the stone he's not suddenly changed in his sentiment, but it is in a state of troubled heart, a groaning natural spirit and still deeply moved that he prays!

> "Father, I thank thee that thou hast heard me. And I knew that thou hearest me always: but because of the people which stand by I said it, that they may believe that thou hast sent me."

That he says, "I thank thee that thou hast heard me" indicates he had already asked his Father for this miracle *before* this prayer.

This is at least the second time Christ has petitioned his Father – and he is thankful that his first petition was heard.

> And when he thus had spoken, he cried with a loud voice, "Lazarus, come forth."

We come out of a spiritual death because of what our Lord Jesus Christ has done. Because of the petitions he made by his words, in his actions and in his life – we are free of the bondage and burden of death – through his life we *have* life. This is something that should move us very much in each and every prayer!

Open your heart – open your mouth

One of my favourite verses in the Old Testament is in Psalm 81;

> "I am the LORD thy God, which brought thee out of the land of Egypt: open thy mouth wide, and I will fill it."

If ever we have any encouragement from God to petition him, this verse pretty much sums up God's eagerness to hear prayer and willingly provide for us. But it takes an action from us too – 'open your mouth wide'.

This verse also reminds me of the story of George Müller. I'd heard of George a few years ago but recently I came across something he'd actually written himself about his experiences and was surprised to read that he used this exact same phrase from Psalm 81:10! I'd wanted to know more about the life of this extraordinary individual, so I was interested in his side of the story.

For those who've not heard of George Müller he was a man who in the early 1800's set about (almost singlehandedly!) to reform welfare in England, particularly for orphans. When he started there were no such things as orphanages, foster homes and certainly no child welfare support or 'family tax benefit Part A'. A *little* had been done by some of the *big* churches but George wanted to contribute to society and to see that the children were actually cared for.

What subsequently made George Müller well known was that he wanted to realise his vision with God's help. He wanted to demonstrate to the next generation that God does help, God does answer prayer and God does hear petition. And to strengthen his own faith George put this to the test in his life and in his work.

George's secret fundraiser

So George set about raising money for this purpose. He didn't have any funds of his own but he needed a lot of money to get the orphanage started. He gathered some likeminded friends and they took their petition to God in prayer. They decided, at George's insistence, that they would *not* ask anyone else for money.

When we want to raise money for Bible mission or aged care or for preaching work, the first thing we do is put together a nice letter - and send it to *everyone* we know.

But George Müller wasn't going to go about things this way. He had a project and needed a lot of money but wasn't going to ask people for the money – he was going to ask God instead.

Here are a few extracts from George's diary, which I think you'll find interesting:

> "I thought a few moments about these words, and then was led to apply them to the case of the orphan house. It struck me that I had never asked the Lord for anything concerning it, except to know His will respecting its being established or not; and I then fell on my knees, opened my mouth wide, asking him for much. I asked in submission to His will, and without fixing a time when He should answer my petition. I prayed that He would give me a house, i.e., either as a loan, or that someone might be led to pay the rent for one, or that one might be given permanently for this object; further, I asked Him for £1000; and likewise for suitable individuals to take care of the children. Besides this, I have been since led to ask the Lord to put into the hearts of His people to send me articles of furniture for the house, and for clothes for the children. When I was asking the petition I was fully aware what I was doing, i.e., that I was asking for something which I had no natural prospect of obtaining from the brethren whom I know, but which was not too much for the Lord to grant."

A thousand pounds may not sound like much in today's billion-dollar welfare budgets of some governments - but in the early 1800's it was something like 50 years worth of wages! So, how was George's petition progressing?

> "December 10, 1835. -- This morning I received a letter, in which a brother and sister wrote thus:-- "We propose ourselves for the service of the intended Orphan-House, if you think us qualified for it; also to give up all the furniture, etc. which the LORD has given us, for its use;

> and to this without receiving any salary whatever; believing that if it be the will of the LORD to employ us, He will supply all our needs, etc."

So, there's the furniture and its previous owners to boot, and unsalaried - he didn't even ask for that.

> "December 13.-- A brother was influenced this day to give 4s. per week, or £10 8s. yearly, as long as the LORD gives the means; 8s. was given by him as two weeks' subscriptions. To-day a brother and sister offered themselves, with all their furniture, and all the provisions which they have in the house, if they can be usefully employed in the concerns of the Orphan-House."

OK, the money's starting to roll in – and more people. It's surprising how God provides. For an enterprise like George was undertaking, what's better than money? The people who can make it happen!

> "December 17.-- I was rather cast down last evening and this morning about the matter, questioning whether I ought to be engaged in this way, and was led to ask the LORD to give me some further encouragement. Soon after were sent by a brother two pieces of print, the one seven and the other 23 3/4 yards of calico, four pieces of lining, about four yards altogether, a sheet, and a yard measure. This evening another brother brought a clothes horse, three frocks, four pinafores, six handkerchiefs, three counterpanes, one blanket, two pewter salt cellars, six tin cups, and six metal tea spoons, he also brought 3s. 6d. given to him by three different individuals. At the same time he told me that it had been put into the heart of an individual to send to-morrow £100."

Good news George, not a bad week's work. But then again, it's not unusual that the Almighty can get a fair bit done in seven days. That should be enough, George should be happy that such blessing against the odds came in within such a small space of time. Not constant George, 18 months later:

> "June 15, 1837.-- To-day I gave myself once more earnestly to prayer respecting the remainder of the £1000. This evening £5 was given, so that now the whole sum is made up. To the Glory of the LORD, whose I am, and whom I serve, I would state again, that every shilling of this money, and all the articles of clothing and furniture, which have been mentioned in the foregoing pages, have been given to me, without one single individual having been asked by me for anything."

What a great example; someone who petitions God and *then goes and does something* for someone else. Sure, we have a lot of needs that we petition God for in our lives – and He gives us a lot of blessings but petitioning God for the benefit of others makes us spiritually stronger in His sight.

Petitioning for others makes it easier to petition for ourselves

Petitioning for ourselves doesn't make us stronger in our spiritual lives if we don't petition for others also. Just because we can petition God for our own needs doesn't necessarily mean that we can petition effectively for the needs of others.

The act of putting ourselves in the place of another, associating with their situation, feeling as they would feel, empathising with them and expressing this in prayer is a deeply moving spiritual practice. Petitioning God in prayer for others in this way means we are always improving not just prayer for ourselves but the very understanding of the source and motivation of prayer.

Of course, the same is true for our understanding of what is appropriate in prayer. When we are looking at a wider interest, a wider sample of humanity's need and dependence on God we learn perspective and values. Suddenly it's easy to see the place prayer occupies or should occupy in our lives.

Praying about problems

Like Hezekiah, we can spread out on the floor all the letters that that concern us, and kneel before them just as Hezekiah did in 2 Kings 19.

We can spread the bills on the floor, especially the electricity bill. Of course, sitting there with them and praying about them with the heater on full while wearing a T-shirt and shorts doesn't make much sense. But that's just the point, isn't it? For prayer to be of use it has to be collaborative, sensible and responsible on our part.

I can remember twice in my life where I've actually done as Hezekiah did. Once was over a bill, a large one. God's answer: I lost my job! It wasn't long before I found another one, the pay was twice as much and that bill suddenly looked so much smaller. It was a good lesson in having the courage to take the answer as well as make the petition.

The second time I remember was over a letter that had some really bad news. It was so devastating at the time that my reaction probably had more to do with going weak at the knees and almost involuntarily spreading the letter (and myself!) on the floor – and there I prayed. I think it was the only thing I could think to do at the time. God answered that prayer too, again not in the way I expected but in a more life-changing way than I could have envisaged.

I guess these days with most of the communication being electronic, a bit of problem correspondence doesn't have the same physical presence or bearing. There's good and bad in that; good that letters and bills don't hang around and bother us – and bad; in that the method of communication is in a form that is more difficult to distance ourselves from.

We can't put the electronic device in the drawer for a few days while we think and pray what to do about that troublesome message – instead we have to 'carry' it around with us. We have to be mindful of the sticky nature of our connected lifestyles. We have to adjust and improvise as to how we deal with the problems we need to present before God in prayer.

Dare to pray for a whole city

In Psalm 122 we read;

> "Pray for the peace of Jerusalem: they shall prosper that love thee. Peace be within thy walls, and prosperity within thy palaces. For my brethren and companions' sakes, I will now say, Peace be within thee."

We have another example in Jeremiah 29, when prayer was required for another city – can you guess which one?

> "Thus saith the LORD of hosts, the God of Israel, unto all that are carried away captives, whom I have caused to be carried away from Jerusalem unto Babylon; Build ye

houses, and dwell *in them;* and plant gardens, and eat the fruit of them; Take ye wives, and beget sons and daughters; and take wives for your sons, and give your daughters to husbands, that they may bear sons and daughters; that ye may be increased there, and not diminished. And seek the peace of the city whither I have caused you to be carried away captives, and pray unto the LORD for it: for in the peace thereof shall ye have peace."

Jeremiah is recording God's message to pray for the peace of Babylon, so that when they are in Babylon they will have peace there.

What city do you live in? Have you prayed for the peace of your Babylon? Have you while being in that place prayed for the peace of Jerusalem? And desired to see that glorious day when we will meet the Lord – who has petitioned our Heavenly Father for us *wherever* we are.

Praying for a whole city may seem a daunting or even frivolous use of prayer. It seems dramatically impossible. But when we stop and think about it there are more reasons to do so than we first think.

Firstly, the challenge of praying for something so large reveals to us the limitless capacity of prayer – and of course the limitless ability of a God whom we reaffirm to ourselves is able achieve that peace.

Secondly, it defines for us exactly what we are praying for. Are we praying just for peace in our own lives in the place in which we reside? Or are we seeking more, perhaps the conversion of that many people? Do we ask ourselves the question, 'Do I really believe that this whole city won't want to hear my petition for them in the day that Christ returns to change the *whole* world not just one little city?'

Thirdly, we are reminded when we pray *on this scale*, that there have been times when just as much has been done before. We've considered examples from David and Jeremiah – but what about Jonah whose preaching saved a whole city? Jonah, being a case in point, is remarkable in that he didn't want to preach to, convert or even pray for Nineveh because he knew that it was already in God's power and will to convert the whole city!

Another example is of Moses who interceded on behalf of not a city but the whole nation of Israel in the wilderness. Exercising the practice of praying for a city is something we do well to rehearse – it's healthy for our confidence in prayer.

The most powerful of prayers

Pray for more opportunities in your life. Ask God to give you more work for Him! He will always answer this prayer.

Being ready to answer 'for' God is the pinnacle of spiritual enlightenment. It is why God's truth trumps every other religion or so-called spiritual idea. None comes close to the calling that God has for those who know His Word and His purpose.

Being ready to answer the opportunities that arise in our relatively small lives is for most of us a relative thing in itself. How ready is ready? The reality is that for most of us we're always going to be a little bit short of the mark. For many that means doing nothing because they don't feel up to the task. Sadly, and I use the term empathetically, there are far too many people doing far too little. You know it, I know it – and it's never us, it's always someone else.

What actually sets apart the *do*-ers from the mere *be*-ers is this willingness to sincerely pray for opportunities to give a ready answer *for* God. There's no surer way to get God's attention than ask Him for something to do. And there's no surer way than to ask for it and start anyway. For some of us this takes courage, enormous courage sometimes. My nervousness in public situations is dwarfed in my own mind by the situations faced by brothers and sisters who live in countries with repressive regimes.

However, we all recognise there is something each of us can do. For me it may be talking to the people in the offices around work of what I do on Sunday, or writing to motivate or encourage others, or to spend time calling a friend and share a thought or two on Scripture.

I am continually surprised as I learn the myriad of ways in which such service is done - some publically, others quite privately, such as the sister who I've known for years – and who I only just learned has been writing to prisoners for 20 years teaching them of God's Word!

Great examples in Scripture fortify our resolve to be the *do*-ers. Foremost of course is our Lord Jesus Christ, who not yet even knowing us laid down his life for us. Jeremiah initially said he was too young to speak on God's behalf – and who later declared that God's word burned within him so mightily that he couldn't help but tell others of it. Moses, irresolute at the burning bush, became the man who in his 80's thundered down Sinai, smashed an idol and took up a people by the scruff of their stiff necks and dragged them towards the land of promise.

Faithful actions speak. These examples inspire us.

We are going to look at 'answers with God' in our next chapter. In the meantime, ask God to give you more work for Him, open the heart that you want to share fully with Him, pray specifically, pray for others, give your prayer life colour, use the word 'bless' in more of your conversations - and believe it!

~ 5 ~
ANSWERS *with* GOD

It's all about foundations

This final chapter is all about *answers* with God, which you probably noticed already. Perhaps when you first picked up this book some of you thought the sooner we get to this point the better. How does God work? How do we get answers? How do we make prayer powerful?

Hopefully, we have added to our understanding through exploring the things we have, and as to where the real power in prayer is. In looking at answers with God we will draw on this understanding.

The Psalmist says at the end of the Psalm 66;

"Blessed be God, which hath not turned away my prayer."

But the question is, 'Does He answer them?' We have already discovered that God hears all prayer – absolutely, every prayer is heard by God. Sometimes we feel like God doesn't answer our prayers. And sometimes we see situations where God answers a prayer immensely, incomprehensibly more than we ever anticipated He would.

The purpose of this chapter is to understand a little bit more about how and why this happens. Because in doing so we learn more of the mind of God. It would be beneficial to us in our desire to talk more with God, to know our subject, our audience and our relationship so much more.

We have discovered the foundations that we now exercise in our lives as we move forward and grow together before God.

In our first chapter, Talking with God, we spent time examining the *will of God* and how this will affects our relationship with God and our understanding of prayer.

Our will is somewhat like a balloon. We take a balloon, then we blow into the balloon and we huff and puff and make this big bright balloon but we don't have the wherewithal to 'tie it off' – so if we let go of it *'phhffffrrrrr'*, off it goes. That is our will. We may like to think differently from time to time but a cursory search of our past reveals the truth about what we are really like when it comes to controlling or depending on our will. We talk about 'will-power' not because we have it but because we need to exert ourselves just to get a little bit of it!

God's will on the other hand is like a shaft of iron, a rod of steel piercing space as He goes from one side of the universe to the another – an unstoppable, undeviating, definite and driving force. What we need to do is *tie* our balloons to that. And then we are in parallel, we are on the right track with the will of God.

We considered Praise with God and how all praise must *honour God*. Praising God where *He is*, for what *He does*, with everything *we have* and, with what *we have been given*. Did you notice in those four statements that there's two for God and two for us? There are two things that God can do with or without us – and there are two that only we can do. In looking at answers with God this a very good clue as to how prayer works.

In Reflection with God we saw that all prayer must *glorify God*. Another example of this someone who prays for rain – they may be an agriculturist or someone who works the land. 'Please send us rain', they say. And their neighbour is a keen skier and he prays, 'Dear God, please tomorrow, let it snow.' And then the third neighbour down the road is getting ready to pave his driveway, 'God please let it be dry today.' Which prayer does God answer?

The answer is that God will always answer the prayer that glorifies Him. If rain will glorify God then that prayer will be answered before a prayer that does not glorify Him. So in reflection, glorifying God is, or should be, a respected part of how we approach our Heavenly Father – remembering He *is* our Father.

When we considered Petition with God, the foundation there was *dependence on God*. Petition is either supplication for us or intercession for others. Both are petition with God.

Now, when we understand these foundations – the will of God, what honours God, what glorifies God and our dependence on God – we have those four building blocks which we bring together as we consider answers with God, then we comprehend the final principle of *acceptance with God*.

Here they are again:
- The Will of God
- What honours God
- What glorifies God
- Dependence on God
- Acceptance with God

Talking with God means becoming a good listener

As we all know, we don't receive messages personally or directly from God – we don't get email or text messages from God, we don't have letters that come in the mail from Him and

He doesn't knock on our door and say, 'Regarding that thing you were talking to me about yesterday; the answer is...'

But we do receive answers from God and reception from God in a lot of other forms. Of course, the first and foremost of these is His Word. He has put that down for us as an answer long before a question's even asked and I don't need to tell you how much we need to get into that Word and enjoy the great wisdom and the answers that are in there already.

Let's consider an example. Say someone has done something so really terrible, they feel really guilty and are really sorry but they despair that there is no hope for them. There are plenty of people like this; some are even driven to suicide because of this state of mind. Should they pray for forgiveness? Is that possible? The answer is emphatically, "Yes!" How do we know? The answer is *already* in the Bible – the Apostle Peter writes in 2 Peter 3:

> "The Lord is not slow in keeping his promise, as some understand slowness. Instead he is patient with you, **not wanting anyone to perish**, but everyone to come to repentance."

Can we possibly overestimate how important it really is to do daily Bible reading? We really don't know when we're going to need an answer to a prayer that's *already* waiting for a question we have yet to ask – that is the brilliance of God's Word and His mind to *prepare* answers for us in advance!

Imagine, really just imagine, what would it be like to already have these answers (or as many as we can remember) in our own heads – and to live a life with answers? It's true, that's what we can all do with the Word of God 'in' our lives. And not only that; we get to share God's answers with others!

I had a powerful reminder of this a week and a half ago. I had a message from reception:

"A Paul called for you, says he used to work with you, wants you to call him back on [phone number]. Thanks, Sheridan".

So as soon as I finished what I was working on I called him:

JB: Pauly old chap, it's JB, nice to hear from you again.
Paul: Hi JB, I've been looking for your number for ages.
JB: Ha, I've probably had half a dozen numbers since I last saw you. How've you been?
Paul: Not so good actually - I wanted to talk to you about something.
JB: Sure, how can I help?
Paul: It's Mel. She's been diagnosed with terminal cancer. The doctor advised me to have a talk with a priest – and you're the only person I could think of.
JB: [taking deep breath, sending up urgent prayer...]

I've not even seen Paul in ten or so years. He's within easy reach of any number of churches, with any number of counselling services. In any given week he must drive by hundreds of them. Yet, he's by-passed all those and called a 'lay' friend because of his impression as to where *answers* may likely be found.

Now I don't think of myself as a priest (not in the sense he was looking for anyway), and certainly not a counsellor – I'd never attempt advising anyone beyond common sense. I have neither qualifications nor experience in the field and some may argue I'm not all that good at common sense either! But I could listen, I could point him in the right direction and I could of course tell him of my own faith (which was partly what he was looking for).

I could have felt honoured, even proud that Paul had sought me out for assistance with what must be a very tough time for him and his family - instead my feeling was one of relief. Relief that the last impression I left on him was that I might have answers – and my second feeling, a close second behind that, was of what an awesome responsibility God has placed in the hands of a total amateur!

The simple point is that God didn't put us here alone; He put us here to '*be* Him – *to* them.' And more than that, He has *already* blessed us with *all* the answers. And no, that's not a typo – I mean *all* the answers.

We may not think they are all in Scripture – but in one way or another they are there, even if it's in that one phrase, 'Lord, I believe; help thou mine unbelief.'

Talking with God also means becoming a good listener because we receive blessings, answers, benefits from God without number. Sometimes we are not listening or looking for them.

How many times do we ask God to bless us in the morning – yet forget to thank him in the evening, even though the blessings were surprising and obvious? Please don't ask me how many times I've done this – I'm far too embarrassed to tell you.

This reminds me of the story of the man who was once lost in the forest. Later he was describing the experience to a friend, explaining how desperate he was, and how he finally resorted to asking God for help. His friend was very interested in this, so he asked, 'Amazing, tell me – did God answer your prayer?!' He who was lost replied, 'Oh no. Before God even had a chance a guide came along and showed me the path.'

You and I can see that that prayer was answered but the answer wasn't noticed by the man who was lost. We are sometimes 'lost' are we not? And consequently we are used to looking in the forest for the answer – is it down this path, is it down that path – when in fact the answer is *someone* who comes down another path and leads us to salvation. Talking with God means becoming a good listener in our forest.

But there is actually much more to this than simple answers. God is in the business of growing spiritual minds for His glory and His purpose. He is continually redrawing the boundaries, consistently raising the bar to draw us closer to Him. Why is it that the most spiritually minded people we know seem to have more challenges than those who really don't care if God is a constant part of their lives?

There are plenty of examples of this in the Bible. Gideon wasn't much interested in what God had planned for him, so he asked God for a miracle just to make sure; and God gave him a clear and simple answer in the fleece being wet and the floor being dry. Spiritually weak, Gideon asked again the next day – this time that the fleece be dry and the ground wet. God didn't argue with him. It was all that Gideon's spiritual mind could manage, so the fleece was dry, the ground wet and Gideon could move on to the next challenge.

Contrast this with poor old Elijah who was a very spiritually minded and faithful prophet of God. One who regularly communed with God – yet look what he had to go through! He had to flee for his life, doubted his usefulness, asked God to let him die (dark places to be), wandered around for forty days on the strength of one meal, ended up living in a cave, alone, depressed, suffering post traumatic stress disorder having seen his fellow prophets slain – and what did God give Him? A wind that was so strong it broke rocks, an earthquake that made living in a cave most unbearable, a raging fire that cooked pretty much everything around, finally He startled him with a still small voice – and then sent him back to work!

Moses is another example, one of spiritual progression this time. He began his calling when he observed a burning bush. He wasn't even looking for God let alone answers. He was perfectly content with his rather simple, albeit boring, life. So God had to get his attention. Even then Moses wasn't so keen on what God had in mind, coming up with excuse after excuse. It's probably not until he's back face to face with a Pharaoh that he's really got his heart in it. By the end of his life, Moses was the only man ever accorded the honour of being one known to speak as it were, face to face with God as a man speaks with his friend.

So being a good listener is not just a matter for the ears or the eyes – but one for the heart and the mind. If the matter is not clear it is not because we are ignored, but rather we should take it as a compliment that there is more spiritual building being afforded us by God who has *all* the answers – not just the little ones we think are immediately important.

What state are you in?

Sometimes we ask the question in one state and find the answer in another. By state I mean state of mind or state of circumstances, not geographical borders, but there's no reason why that shouldn't happen too. Importantly between the asking and the answering we should have grown. God is very interested in this.

Always expect that between the question and the answer there will be something required of us, and be keen to get into that state and grow that little bit more in the sight of our Heavenly Father. Sometimes this may be growing in faith, patience, wisdom, the intangible but also the most important and valuable.

There's something to be said about knowing that once we have reached this new state we are *already* more valuable to Him. We have grown into the new boots that we didn't ask for, didn't know we needed and certainly were not going to ask for of our own accord!

I know from my own experiences in life, that what I thought I wanted; when I get a little further down the track I then realise I have underestimated or underrated because I am not the same person I used to be and therefore couldn't see myself in that better or mature state. Hence I didn't know what I'd need until I got there.

One of the most frustrating things in life is *hindsight* – where on earth is it when we actually need it?! But then that would make it foresight. I will confess, I'm really good at seeing things in hindsight and saying, 'I'm glad I know now what I didn't know then.'

But when it comes to applying what I *should* know, or what I *should* see about the state I am in now compared to where I *should* be – I tend to ignore it and it usually falls to God to pick up the trailing cord and give me a tug in the right direction. My nature is to stop, to settle, to stay and dare I say it even to atrophy a little bit too.

God is perfect, absolutely one hundred percent perfect. There are no improvements to be made to His character or His spirituality or His being. Yet God is *never* still. What on earth makes me think it's perfectly fine if I am?!

Yes and No

'Yes' is definitely an answer to many prayers, and 'yes' is sometimes found in listening a different way. We can do ourselves an enormous favour and *allow* God to answer in His way – chances are He knows best.

Sometimes God's answer to prayer is 'No.' As humans we can say 'no' to a lot of things, our parents taught us that! But sometimes we get a bit unstuck on this logic when we take a prayer or petition to God and say, 'God, answer this' or 'Can I have that' or 'Please give me this' and expect an entirely different logic to apply. 'No' is a valid word in the divine vocabulary as it is in the mortal one.

Sometimes our Father knows it is in our best interest to answer 'No.' Just as your children or your friends and family might ask a question of you – you too can say 'no'. We have good reasons most of the time for saying 'no'. We can rest assured that our Heavenly Father's reasons do not contain any of those elements that we have in our minds or in our lives that are tainted or touched with envy or deceit or jealousy or any other reason *we* might decline an offer. God's motives and God's mind, and God's answers will always be pure – and sometimes for His will, honour, glory or our dependence the best answer is 'No'.

I remember several desperate occasions in my life where I have asked for something that could not possibly be interpreted as anything other than a totally justified, perfectly reasonable question, a perfectly reasonable petition, 'Please give me…' - and the answer has been, 'No'. At these times I felt a lot of emotions - satisfaction not being one of them.

In hindsight I can look back at these now and say, 'I'm so glad the answer was no. I wouldn't be where I am in my life now spiritually, or financially, or by any other measure I can think of if the answer back then had been 'yes'. Hindsight admittedly is a wonderful thing – but when in the moment we are staring down the barrel of a difficult problem or we've got difficult choices ahead of us, it does seem difficult to hear 'no'. Chances are you can think of one such situation right now.

'No' is an answer with God. That doesn't mean we are happy accepting the 'no' – but that's OK, we are allowed to reason with God. He knows what we are like, He says, "Yes, I know, I'm going to tell him 'no', and he's going to say 'why not?' – but when he says 'why not?' or when she says 'how come?' they are going to have to think and come up with a reason as to why the answer is like it is – and in doing so they will draw a little closer to me. In the meantime I'm going to keep them out of *long-term* trouble and I'm going to answer 'no'."

Wait

'Yes' and 'no' are both answers but the most interesting answer of all, perhaps one of the most intriguing is found in that little word, 'wait.'

Sometimes God says yes to a petition, sometimes no and these may come in a whole range of forms. Answers are not always immediate, simple or straightforward. In fact, almost every time we have a yes or no in our lives as a concerted answer to our prayers they are very much over days, weeks, months, even years of ongoing or parallel activity. It's not an easy thing to accept, I know believe me – but sometimes the answer to prayer is 'wait.'

Because God knows that we are not ready for a yes, and we're also not prepared for a no, He wants something else for us. He wants something better for us. Let me ask you an important question: as we walk towards the hope of the return of the Lord Jesus Christ, and the setting up of the Kingdom on earth, what are we doing? We are waiting.

Let me ask you another question - which thing in your life could you petition God about that would not be fixed or changed, would not be answered if the Kingdom of God was on earth right now?

Think about it. Let's say I want a new job, and I take that petition to God, 'God, I need that new job, please answer my prayer.' And I prayed that on Monday. The answer was on its way Tuesday but I didn't get it then because the company advertising the job had sent us a letter by post and I wouldn't receive that letter until Wednesday. But now on Wednesday the Kingdom of God arrived and I never found out if I got that job or not. Would I be disappointed? No way!

'Wait' is an answer with God. Remember, it is both in our power now and also within our experience of the past to wait. Nothing we have in this life is a problem, a challenge, a rebuttal, a debate, a stalling, a yes or no or anything else will ever be too big to be answered when the Kingdom of God arrives. It's the answer to all problems and all petitions.

'God, please take away my arthritis' – Kingdom of God; fixed, no more arthritis. 'Dear Heavenly Father, my great-aunt is on her deathbed, please give her peace, and please strengthen her' – along comes the Kingdom of God; and that is fixed also. We are waiting for the Kingdom of God now. Build *waiting* into your petition as an expectation because 'wait' *is* an answer.

Here's another visual that you can probably relate to. There was a time in my life where I had an important question for God. I really had it in my head that it needed answering 'right now' – it didn't but I thought it did. They cast lots in the Bible so I wondered if tossing a coin may make it clearer to my mind - heads 'yes', tails 'no.'

Against my better judgement I flipped the coin. It was heads – 'yes'. And then my brain slowly started to stir back to life. Should I toss the coin to see if I should do it 'now'? My gambling experiences are rather limited but even I knew it was statistically probable that the next toss would not be heads – my tricky mind toyed with the idea of 'if it lands on *tails* this time it means yes to *now*'. And if it doesn't... I stood there looking at the coin and it began to dawn on me – there is no way to toss this coin for 'when'. I put the coin back in my pocket and got on with *waiting*.

Waiting is very much a part of answers with God. In fact, I would go so far as to say that it is even more important than a yes or no answer because it demands more of us spiritually and therefore contributes greatly to our character.

Here is a short poem, which is actually simply called 'Wait'. It was penned by Russell Kelfer, and it really does speak to the heart of what we know to be true of this *waiting*.

WAIT

Desperately, helplessly, longingly I cried;
quietly, patiently, lovingly God replied.
I pled and I wept for a clue to my fate,
and the Master so gently said, "Child you must wait."
Wait? You say, wait? my indignant reply.
Lord, I need answers, I need to know why!

Is your hand shortened? Or have you not heard?
By faith, I have asked, and am claiming your Word.
My future and all to which I can relate
hangs in the balance and you tell me to WAIT?
I'm needing a "yes," a go-ahead sign,
or even a "no" to which I can resign.

And Lord, you promised that if we believe
we need but to ask, and we shall receive.
And Lord, I've been asking, and this is my cry,
I'm weary of asking, I need a reply!

Then quietly, softly, I learned of my fate
as my Master replied once again, "You must wait."
So, I slumped in my chair, defeated and taut
and grumbled to God, so I'm waiting....for what?
He seemed then to kneel, and His eyes wept with mine,
and He tenderly said, "I could give you a sign.
I could shake the heavens and darken the sun,
I could raise the dead and cause mountains to run.
All you seek I could give, and pleased you would be.
You would have what you want, but you would not see.

You'd not know the depth of My love for each saint,
You'd not know the power that I give to the faint.
You'd not learn to see through the clouds of despair,
You'd not learn to trust just by knowing I'm there.

You'd not know the joy of resting in Me,
when darkness and silence were all you could see.
You'd never experience that fullness of love
as the peace of My Spirit descends like a dove.
You'd know that I give and I save...(for a start),
but you'd not know the depth of the beat of My heart.

> The glow of My comfort late into the night.
> The faith that I give when you walk without sight.
> The depth that's beyond getting just what you asked
> of an infinite God, who makes what you have last.
> You'd never know, should your pain quickly flee,
> what it means that "My grace is sufficient for thee."
> Yes, your dreams for your loved one overnight would come true,
> but, oh the loss, if I lost what I'm doing in you!
>
> So, be silent, My child, and in time you will see,
> that the greatest of gifts is to get to know Me.
> And though oft' My answers seem terribly late,
> My most precious answer of all is still, Wait.

Waiting is an answer. Waiting is something that we *do* in this state that we find ourselves in as we walk towards the Kingdom of God - when all answers will be made evident. We are blessed in the meantime to be able to talk with God and to be able to have Him listen, in reading, by petition, by prayer, by praise and by reflection.

Remember the incident Paul tells about himself in 2 Corinthians 12;

> "For this thing I besought the Lord thrice, that it might depart from me. And he said unto me, My grace is sufficient for thee: for my strength is made perfect in weakness. Most gladly therefore will I rather glory in my infirmities, that the power of Christ may rest upon me."

We see as we wait, that we therefore glory in the grace of God now. Grace isn't something we turn on or off with a tap. It's not something that we get up in the morning and say, 'God, I'm about to start the day, I've been asleep all night, can you give me some more grace to start my day'. Grace was given *once* as we know it and so we should refer to it in this way, I sometimes hear it describes in multitude, when for this I think they mean blessings. 'Once' our Lord Jesus Christ made open the way by which we can approach our Heavenly Father. Being immersed in his sin covering Name and walking by *sight* in faith as we do now - we live and walk in the glory of that grace *now*.

It's not mercy (that we need at other times), grace is *always* upon us as we have learnt. As soon as we understand the grace that we have in Jesus Christ we are never, ever without it. Now was that a 'yes' before we even asked that question or not! Paul was given the answer, 'My grace is sufficient to thee' – it *always is* for us too.

Spend time listening

Sometimes we 'rush off' a prayer to God and say in essence, 'Oh God I need this, so you go and fix that and I'm going to go and deal with this'. And even the most pious of us have been guilty of treating prayer like this. It's better to spend time listening to God. James talks about this, where he comments about the incident where Elijah, being a man subject to like passions as we are, in other words someone who was *exactly* like us – had to learn prayer, learn patience and learn obedience. James says:

> "Elias was a man subject to like passions as we are, and he prayed earnestly that it might not rain: and it rained not on the earth by the space of three years and six months. And he prayed again, and the heaven gave rain, and the earth brought forth her fruit."

For those of you who are praying for rain I hope you don't have to wait three years for it. Some parts of planet earth are in drought and many people can relate to that. Elijah wouldn't be popular today if he was up to that again – but as a man just like us, he is someone who *exercised* prayer and in this he is a good example.

We need to spend time listening not just to God but to ourselves. Like me you've probably had moments of realisation when I couldn't believe I'd just prayed for that – or worse I'd just prayed and I didn't remember a word I just said. We can *tune out* of our own mindfulness. It's our nature to be absent minded or as is often the case, distracted.

In times past, although I expect it is still done by some today, fasting, or denying one's own good, focused the mind on prayer. I can see how it can work and there are examples in Scripture, generally however, I think it is an *unsustainable* practice. I use the word 'practice' deliberately because prayer is talking with God but it is also an exercise – a spiritual exercise. We need that exercise for spiritual strength our *entire lives*, not just forty days and forty nights – we're not all like Elijah or Jesus.

Fasting may focus the mind for a short while but is better for us to practise listening *long-term* and strengthen this exercise in our prayers. Have you asked yourself what you pray for most often? What do you think about while praying? Do we visualise those spiritual things we hope for?

The Word of answers

As we've considered, many prayers are already answered in the Word. We cannot stress enough how opening the Word, drawing upon the lives of these faithful men and women of old gives us so many of those answers that we are looking for now. We need to do this daily, we need that spiritual input and we need to get as many of those examples and experiences in our mind and in our life as possible. Why? Because when the questions come along we'll have something to draw on because the spiritual bank account has something in it. Open the Word – there is so much answered in there already.

In fact here's an exercise for you. Use a blue pencil, I always say in pencil because you may want to do something else later, and draw an outline around all the prayers in your Bible – particularly those concerned with petition. Then shade in all the answers to those prayers in blue. I wouldn't be surprised if you found that you had more shaded in boxes than outlines - because almost every prayer in the Bible is answered.

Sometimes it's yes, sometimes no, and sometimes wait (Abraham is a good example of 'wait' that comes to mind). But if you do this exercise in blue pencil it will give you some confidence as to how God answers prayers – and those answers are already in His Word.

The Rewarder

God is the *rewarder* of those who look to Him. For those who desire to see His will achieved God is very rewarding, very generous in His giving.

I think that one of the lowest times in my life was when I asked God to give me peace. It was during troublesome times in business, too much was happening, there were too many demands on me – many of which I felt inadequate or inexperienced to deal with. All the hassle left me almost no time for anything else in my life, including those things which were spiritual. God in His wisdom decided to teach me a lesson and granted my prayer!

If you've never experienced this sort of situation let me tell you, not much happens in peace; not much gets done, not much gets answered and not much gets sought after – it's like a vacuum of everything. Yes it might be a vacuum of those things that were stressing me out at the time but it's also a vacuum of all those things that were good for me and that *challenged* me. And that's where so many answers are found. Contentment is perhaps healthy for us but peace and a lack of challenges, and of opportunities is not!

God is a rewarder of those who diligently seek Him. Ask for the gift but expect the giver. Abraham did that. Have a look at Hebrews chapter 11. You know these words well,

> "But without faith it is impossible to please him: for he that cometh to God must believe that he is, and that he is a rewarder of them that diligently seek him. By faith Abraham, when he was called to go out into a place which he should after receive for an inheritance, obeyed; and he went out, not knowing whither he went. For he looked for a city which hath foundations, whose builder and maker is God."

That's what Abraham looked for. Abraham wasn't looking for vast herds of cattle and plains of pasture with a big mansion that he was going to build with his family. Abraham sought God in the equation – not the wealth. The wealth came, that was answered in many other ways. But Abraham looked for the giver of the reward not the reward itself – and that is why God blessed him so richly in his life.

Abraham was comfortable in Ur of the Chaldees. He had a great time there, he was wealthy, he had a very good life, he didn't need anything, Abraham appreciated God and what God was doing for him – but he wasn't challenging himself. Abraham didn't know it but God did and so He challenged Abraham to something better, something greater – to create an entire nation for His glory.

God's zone

God had something for Abraham. Hence Abraham sought God and so he moved out of his comfort zone and went to God's zone. Likewise we, in petitioning God and searching for answers with God need to be ready, *always* ready, always prepared for an answer that demands more of us than we first thought.

It's in the young couple who pray to God that they may have children, and they get twins. It's in the young brother and the young sister, who ask God to give them an assembly where they can grow and contribute in their life and walk before him and He gives them a little assembly in an out-of-the-way place with a lot of enthusiasm and a lot of work to be done. It's in the little guy who prays for a promotion and on the next day get's asked a question about God from the boss.

That's how God works, that's what He wants for us – to bring us to the next level, to bring us into a zone out of our comfort zone and into one that honours Him, glorifies Him and leaves us dependent on him. He deliberately brings us and everybody else we come into contact with, to a place where the will of God is carried forward and is made to shine because one person, two people, a few people prayed that God would give them *opportunity*. He is the God of just that state – and He wants *you* in it!

It takes character and courage, experience and trust, to put ourselves, literally, at the mercy of God. He wants to look at us and smile that divine and knowing smile; to say "I remember the day I created you. I remember teaching you to walk, you practised listening to me, and I delighted in teaching you. You used to ask me for things and doubt me – now you don't ask for anything but to be closer to me. You trust Me, I love you and I have more for you."

Live inside a prayer

Do you want to learn a really powerful spiritual exercise? Learn to say, 'My life is not a dream – my life is a prayer.' Imagine a dream life in which everything you had comprised that life – you could live the perfect day you wanted, had the perfect house, perfect kids, perfect spouse, job, car, clothes, body, friends, health, neighbours and let's even throw in perfect mother-in-law. Many people, including me cannot even begin to imagine this – let alone hope for it.

But whoever we are, we can say and imagine; 'My life *is* a prayer.' We can have this prayer because God grants just such prayers. It is a life where everything relates to God, His will and our lives. We are always safe inside a prayer. We are certain and assured. Our thoughts and desires are pure and right inside a prayer.

Augustine said,

> "For your desire is your prayer; and your desire is without ceasing; your prayer will also be without ceasing."

He elaborates from the words of Paul;

> "Pray without ceasing."

The concept I'd like to leave with you, having shared this small journey together in discovering these wonderful foundations of talking with God is that you *can* live inside a prayer.

That's the ultimate goal for any prayer *life*. To pray for health and live a healthy life. To pray for challenges and to meet them with faith. To ask for a more spiritual life, to read more and understand more of His Word. To ask a purpose for yourself and to act on it. To ask a prayer for someone else and then go and do something just for them.

All these things that we've been considering and thinking about here in this theme of Talking with God is actually *living* a prayer life. Now you have the opportunity to take that further and live inside that prayer – *your* prayer.

Imagine how much easier it is for you to communicate with your Heavenly Father *in* there.

Look at these words from Philippians. Writing these wonderful words to some very close friends the Apostle Paul was excited about their hope and future. So he said,

> "Rejoice in the Lord alway: and again I say, Rejoice. Let your moderation be known unto all men. The Lord is at hand. Be careful for nothing; but in *every thing by prayer* and supplication with thanksgiving let your requests be made known unto God. And the peace of God, which passeth all understanding, shall keep your hearts and minds through Christ Jesus."

Look at those points:

- Be careful for nothing; but in everything by prayer – *this is reflection with God*
- And supplication – *this is petition with God*
- And thanksgiving – *this is praise with God*

Now is the time, the best time, to begin talking with God. Praise, reflection, petition - build them into your life. Pray continually.

Above all; look for God in every answer – and look for every answer in God.

www.ingramcontent.com/pod-product-compliance
Lightning Source LLC
Chambersburg PA
CBHW061652040426
42446CB00010B/1696